CUT THE CRAP & MOVE TO COSTA RICA

CUT THE
CRAP
&
MOVE TO
COSTA RICA

A How-to Guide Based
on These Gringos' Experience

Steve & Nikki Page

Viva Purpose
912 Rocky Mountain Way
Fort Collins, CO 80526
http://vivapurpose.com

Printed in the United States of America
26 25 24 23 22 21 20 19 18 17   1 2 3 4 5

ISBN-13 (hardcover): 978-0-9993506-3-8
ISBN-13 (paperback): 978-0-9993506-0-7
ISBN-13 (ebook): 978-0-9993506-1-4

Table of Contents

Follow Us On Social Media

Website: http://cutthecrapcostarica.com/
Facebook: https://www.facebook.com/CutTheCrapCR/
Instagram: https://www.instagram.com/Cutthecrapcostarica
YouTube: https://www.youtube.com/channel/UCHvnt-zoTbHShih2NSvhgWQ
Pinterest: https://www.pinterest.com/bedcd82afac6be4326022d77b1bf41/overview/

Dedication

To our parents, thank you for understanding why we needed to take this journey. We know it was hard when we took the grandbabies away. We thank God every day for the roles you play in our lives and each of our children's' lives. Your lessons are the wisdom that has allowed us to navigate life.

To our eldest Chance, you amaze us every day. Your eye for capturing the beauty of this world has taught us to experience life from new perspectives. It's been an honor to work with you on a professional level. We are excited to be a part of your next step.

To our daughter Morgan, you kind heart helps the sun shine brighter every day. You remind us that we should not let the doubts of others keep us from taking our own path. We are so proud of the women you have become. Never give up on your dreams.

To our son Ellis, thank you for the sacrifices you made for this dream to be possible. Your humor has brought relief to the darkest days. We are so proud of the man you have become. We can't wait to see what you do with your entrepreneurship.

To our youngest Taya, thank you for showing us how important it was to get our book published in hardcover for our readers. As you leave the nest and fly on your own remember to dream big because you can do anything. We will always be your biggest fans.

To our readers and community, we can't say thank you enough. You made our dreams of becoming worldwide bestsellers come true. The love and support have been amazing! We look forward to working with you on the next step of your adventure.

Disclosure

*C*ut the Crap & Move to Costa Rica is based on our experiences with some additional research added in. We must disclose that we are not attorneys, accountants, travel experts, or therapists. Please understand that we are common people who feel that our experiences have yielded some educational understanding about relocating to the tropical paradise known as Costa Rica. This book is not necessarily an instruction manual of what you *should* do but rather an overview of what we have done. We are simply a North American gringo (a person, especially an American, who is not Hispanic or Latino) family that took a risk and found a fountain of experience.

Because we are from the United States, the way we report our experiences will have the perspective of someone coming from the U.S., such as our use of U.S. dollars, the difference in climate, and the local customs that differ from what we are accustomed to. Understandably, our past lives are the lenses we look through as we discover the differences in our current environment. These understandings of where we have come from and how they differ from our new atmosphere are where we have found the value and interest that we wish to share with others who may be considering embarking on a life-changing journey.

Some may criticize that we are "rookies" in Costa Rica and, therefore, not qualified as experts. We submit the opposite. Our expertise lies in the perspective of people who, with limited knowledge and understanding of the culture and environment they would be facing, made the choice to jump headfirst into the deep end. We recently relocated to Costa Rica and know what that experience is like currently, not a decade ago.

Our recommendations for services are based on our personal experiences, and we have included those business and organization websites, when available, in the back of the book.

Who Are Steve and Nikki?

We are a couple in our early 40s who, at the beginning of this journey, had two teenage children at home. Our son was sixteen when we moved here, and his sister was twelve. In addition, we have two adult daughters who stayed behind in the United States. We currently live in Tamarindo, Costa Rica, which was our first stop in this country. We have explored the western part of the country from the Nicaraguan border to the Osa Peninsula as well as the northern Central Valley, San Jose, and over to Limon. We chose the Tamarindo area due to its beautiful beaches and large expat community, which we felt was the key to a smooth transition during our first couple years.

Why Did We Choose Change?

All but one member of our family was born in the same hospital of the same city in Colorado. We lived within a thirty-mile radius of where we were born our entire lives. The only exception was for Steve while he served in the Navy. We were accustomed to the climate and culture of our Colorado community, which is a paradise of its own; however, we needed change and a new start. We had fallen into ruts with our way of life and our relationships. Our children didn't seem to be learning anything new, and our lifestyle had trapped us.

We tried many things to fix our issues, including therapy, time together, time apart, and just plain sucking it up. Nothing was working, and the cycles seemed to perpetuate. We just couldn't seem to move beyond a certain point and would return to our same habits and standstills. Small changes weren't working, so we thought, "How about a drastic one?" The most extreme path is what we chose — sell everything, liquidate our life, quit our jobs, and move away from all we knew. We were going to be our own support system.

We left the U.S. and arrived in Costa Rica with a total of sixteen bags, including two large suitcases, one backpack, and one personal bag each. In the two years since our move, we have accumulated considerably more both from local purchases and additional items brought from the States through friends visiting and our visits home.

So what happened to all of our stuff in the United States? Because we chose to take the leap with both feet and a "no return" plan, we sold almost everything. Did we test the water first? Nope. But of course, we visited Costa Rica several times, right? Nope. We just went for it with no plan B.

We don't want to give the wrong impression. Our move was not some flippant decision to throw caution to the wind and gamble our future with no idea what we were doing. We (and by we I mean Nikki) spent several months researching Costa Rica. We searched the web for everything from health care to housing and from climate to culture. After months of research, we reached a point where we were having trouble finding new books, articles, blogs, or sites with information that we hadn't already uncovered. We had to make a decision, and as far as we could tell, the best way to find out if moving would work was to try it.

We sold our home, two cars, sports equipment, tools, and whatever other items we could. We were a middle-class family, and, aside from our liquidation, we had minimal funds in savings. The money from our liquidation sale became our relocation nest egg that would be necessary to establish our life in our new environment. After selling everything we could, we each kept one trunk in storage of whatever special items we wanted to save. Everything else was donated or given away. Steve, who is a bit of a pack rat, struggled while watching the stuff he spent good money for, that still worked perfectly, get distributed with no compensation for its value. To him, it just felt wrong, and all Nikki could say was "Let it go, let it go, let it go" over and over again.

To make our house look sale ready, we staged it by removing everything but the bare essentials (beds, TVs, and minimal furniture) and what was packed in our suitcases to move. This process required strict deadlines for items to be gone. We had specific dates set for specific items to be sold by, and we held fast to the deadlines. This was a very enlightening place to be. We were releasing almost all of our possessions; all of the wealth we had accumulated over the years was being liquidated. The sum of our labor and toil was reduced to a number in a bank account that hardly seemed worth the sacrifice to achieve it. However, that was it—we had our nest egg.

The day our house went under contract, Steve quit his job, and we booked our tickets. We had thirty days to tie up all loose ends and prepare for our one-way trip.

Why Tamarindo?

Honestly, we chose Tamarindo, Costa Rica, because that was where our first hotel was, plus we fell in love with the area and haven't found a better fit yet. Before we moved, we knew we wanted to live somewhere with a beach since a beach is a contrast to the mountains where we are from. When booking our flights, it was cheaper to fly into the smaller Costa Rican city of Liberia than the capital of San Jose located in the heart of the country. Also, Liberia wasn't far from the coast, and we knew we didn't want to be in a large city like San Jose. From research, we thought the northern coastal region of Guanacaste where we were flying into would be the best place for us to start since it has less of a rainy season and a large expatriate community. (Expats are people living in one country with citizenship from another.)

Although our ultimate goal was full immersion, we felt the large English-speaking population would ease our culture shock and allow us to establish ourselves better which in turn would increase our chances of a successful transition. Our choice has proven to be a wise choice. The Tamarindo area, although more expensive than other areas of the country, is a great middle ground between the United States way of life and the tico way of the natives.

RECOMMENDATION

We booked our initial stay at Hotel Villa Amarilla because it had good reviews on Trip Advisor with no reports of water issues or bugs that were common in many other hotels. This stay at the Hotel Villa Amarilla was the tropical paradise escape we were looking for. With beautifully decorated rooms, this boutique hotel offered a relaxing environment with the beach located on the other side of the gate. This was exactly what we needed for our first five days following an extremely stressful move while maintaining our budget.

What Is It Like?

Tamarindo is on the "Gold Coast" in northern Costa Rica where there is much less rain than other areas of Costa Rica. The temperature in Tamarindo stays between 24° and 40° Celsius (75° – 105° Fahrenheit). Most days the temperature stays around 32° – 37° C (in the 90s F). December to May, the days are dry with no rain and few clouds. January and February have strong warm winds that come down from Nicaragua and shoot out to sea through Tamarindo. From May through August we experience occasional rain a couple times a week, mostly in the evenings and at night. September through November is considered the rainy season in Tamarindo with thunderstorms likely most days. For few weeks during those months, the rain does not stop; however, many days are sunny in the morning with showers and thunderstorms throughout the afternoon and night.

Our favorite time of year is June and July when the rain returns. The landscape explodes with green vegetation and flowers of every color imaginable. When it does rain, it is a warm rain, and people still swim and surf in the ocean as long as there is no lightning.

Playa Tamarindo (Tamarindo Beach) is a mile of golden sand beach with fine soft sand. At one end is an estuary where you can find a wide variety of shells, but watch out for the crocodiles. (Seriously, people have lost limbs since our arrival. Don't freak out because it was the human's fault for not heeding warnings and his ignorance to the area.) The other end of the beach is a rocky point that separates Playa Tamarindo from Playa Langosta. (Steve found a baby leatherback turtle in need of rescue at this end.) Playa Tamarindo is a great beach for surfing, hanging out, and having dinner while watching the sunset on the water. At low tide, we have seen puffer fish, octopus, and jellyfish in the tide pools along with various minnows, crabs, sand dollars, and starfish.

The roads throughout Tamarindo vary in quality. The

road from the airport to the center of town is paved but watch out for potholes that may not have been there the last time. Outside of the main drive through Tamarindo, the roads are dirt with conditions varying from fresh grade to severely rutted, as in you may get high centered with not all of your tires touching the road at the same time. Most roads are quite narrow. When the road is marked "Prohibido Estacionar" (No Parking), it seems to be a suggestion. People often stop in the middle of the road to get out of the car and go into the shops to buy something or handle whatever business they need.

Although most of the time major congestion is not an issue, during high season and especially during the weeks of Christmas and New Year's, walking through Tamarindo can feel like a real-life game of Frogger. Driving can feel like a game of Grand Theft Auto with motorcycles weaving between traffic and cars passing within centimeters of rubbing paint as drivers fold in mirrors to get by.

Very few sidewalks or bike paths exist, so the sides of the narrow streets are cluttered with walkers and bikers and occasionally children and dogs. Since cars are very expensive here and wages are so low, people ride bikes or walk. As a motorist, this can be problematic as pedestrians often wear dark clothes making it difficult to spot them on the road. During the day, many locals can be seen walking from the bus stops to their place of work or children in their uniforms to school.

Amazingly, through this chaos, the locals here have found a way to flow through the streets in harmony with very few incidences of accidents. Road rage seems not to exist. Horns are honked to say "hola" to friends or to let someone know they have space to move. The sounds and the commotion of traffic can be a bit overwhelming at first, but, after a while, it just becomes a way of life and you learn how things flow. We discuss Road Conditions more thoroughly in its own section later on.

Do You Need to Learn Spanish?

If you are an English speaker, which we are going to assume you are since this book is written in English, you should be able to "survive" without learning Spanish. That being said, Spanish is the national language, and if you plan to live in this nation, we recommend you learn the language. Most tourist areas have a high English-speaking population of both expats and natives; however, if you travel outside these areas, you will find fewer bilingual people. If you speak only English, your challenges will increase when trying to adjust to the new culture. In the tourist areas, the ticos or natives would rather speak English so they can practice; plus it's easier for them to understand than our broken Spanish.

Every smartphone has downloadable apps to translate whatever you want to say into whatever language you want to say it in. Although this technology can be very useful, it is not always accurate and takes **way too long**. Often the translation software will give you a word that does not directly mean what you are trying to say. Hopefully, the person you are communicating with can use clues to figure out what you are talking about, but once again, it takes a long time to communicate a simple thought. An additional issue of using apps as your communication crutch is that some applications do not work offline or must be downloaded for offline use. We still use the apps on our phones at times, but we recognize the limits of these tools and realize that learning the language is far superior.

We recommend that you learn some basic Spanish before you come or have a plan to learn upon arrival. Either way, life will be easier if you can speak the language. If you are trying to get a start before leaving the U.S., we recommend checking with a local university or community college for class offerings. Some communities also offer Spanish lessons through the local school district. Once you are in Costa Rica, several options exist for learning Spanish.

RECOMMENDATION

Another option is taking online classes or purchasing software for your computer. While Nikki is still searching for the method of learning that best suits her, Steve has found the free app and website Duolingo most effective in teaching him this new language. Practicing on the app along with using what he has learned while shopping, paying bills, and interacting with people in the community has developed his ability to communicate in most situations without the need of an interpreter or translation app on his phone.

WHAT TO BRING

When deciding what items to bring with you, the major considerations are cost and availability of items here versus where you are coming from. (The Hard-to-Find or Expensive Products section in the Shopping chapter lists some of the items you may consider bringing due to these concerns.) In the end, much of what you bring will depend on which items you "can't live without" or can't replace here. Remember, for many this move is a chance to simplify your life so bringing a bunch of "baggage" from your old life may be prohibitive to that end.

The following is a list of items we found helpful to bring from the States.

1. **Any electronics you use**

   Electronics are extremely expensive, and selection is limited.

   a. **Unlocked Cell Phones**

      4G or later are preferred. If the phone is unlocked, you can use local pre-pay cellular service. (See the Telephone section in the Utilities chapter for more information.)

b. **TVs**

We packed two 32" televisions in our luggage. This may not be a priority for some, but we enjoy watching television in bed. TVs are expensive here, and most homes do not have a bedroom TV. So far, our rentals have only offered one television in the living room.

c. **Quality Camera**

You may be thinking that you'll simply use your smartphone's camera, but that may not be enough. If you do some exploring, you will encounter beautiful sights that you may wish to capture and share. Cameras are available in Costa Rica, but they are pricey, and selection is limited.

d. **Game Console and/or Casting Device**

We use Netflix daily and use either Chromecast or our PS3s to play it on the TV. We also enjoy gaming from time to time. We even use online gaming to stay in contact with our older kids in the States. This has increased the frequency of hearing from them, so we stay in touch better.

2. **Kitchen Appliances and Utensils**

Options and selection for appliances are limited in Guanacaste. Specifically, we recommend you shop for what you like and bring the following small appliances:

a. **Juicer**

b. **Pressure cooker/slow cooker**

c. **Pineapple slicer**

We brought along a metal one that is much better than the plastic ones available here.

d. **Strong plastic or wood spoons**

e. **Hot water kettle**

For making tea, instant soups, and coffee. We use the Costa Rican method of pouring hot water through a cloth "sock" of coffee grounds to make our coffee.

f. **Measuring Cups/Spoons**

Surprisingly difficult to find.

g. **Meat thermometer**

3. **Hygiene Items**

See the Hard-to-Find or Expensive Products section in the Shopping chapter for a list of prices.

4. **First-Aid Kit and Medicine**

We brought the staple items from our medicine cabinet. We didn't want to arrive and have an emergency before we had a chance to locate the pharmacy or a grocery store that was open. Diarrhea can happen suddenly, and many first-aid items are expensive as well.

5. **Lightweight Clothing**

When planning your wardrobe, the first consideration is light-weight and quick-drying clothing to work well in the hot humid climate. Another consideration is finding your style here, which may be difficult. In the beach towns, bikinis and swimsuits are suitable, if not standard attire, even in most restaurants. Shoes are optional most places in coastal towns. Once you leave the beach, it is a different story. You will find very few people not wearing at least shorts and tank tops. Some locals wear pants or jeans, and several lose the flip-flops and opt for tennis shoes or high heels.

6. **Raincoat**

    A quality raincoat can make your life much more comfortable in the rainy season and when you take trips into the rainforest/cloudforest.

Bonus Items

The following is a list of items that we found to be extremely important to us.

1. **Hard Plastic Suitcases**

    We purchased a couple sets of hard suitcases with the four pivoting casters and bright colored zippers. These cases protected our electronics and breakables in transport, and the free rotating wheels on all corners made them much easier to maneuver through the airport. Ours even had TSA locks allowing us to keep them locked in transport.

2. **Towels**

   We ordered quick-dry microfiber towels from Amazon.com that we love. Although thick heavy towels sound very comfortable, they are extremely difficult to dry (especially in rainy season). Thick towels also hold a ton of sand which then fills your washer and dryer.

3. **Bed Sheets**

   (If you know the size of bed) Finding quality sheets can be difficult and expensive.

4. **Tools**

   If you plan to work on any hobbies or are buying a place that you would like to work on yourself, quality tools are expensive, and the selection is very limited.

What Not to Bring

In addition to informing you of what to bring, we thought it would be good to tell you about things you should consider **not** bringing.

1. **Photo Albums**

   We recommend you bring copies of photos that are special but leave the originals elsewhere. The humid climate degrades photos over time, and you do not want to lose those precious memories. We scanned our photos, stored the originals at a family member's house, and play the digital photos on our computer.

2. **Book Collection**

If you are an avid reader, we would suggest getting used to the digital world and utilizing services such as Kindle or Nook. The issue is, once again, the environment. Mold is a real concern throughout the country, especially during rainy season. A small bookstore in Tamarindo sells new and used books. For the avid reader, this may be beneficial and allow for leaving more books behind in the States. If you have valuable books or those that hold sentimental value, we recommend they not move with you.

3. **Leather Items**

Even in the driest part of the country like where we are in Guanacaste, the levels of humidity are high. This is problematic for leather items. We have battled mold on most of our leather items including the couches in our rental home and the shoes and belts in the closet. We even had a leather-covered Bible in its original box with a plastic window. The window stuck to the leather and peeled the top surface of the leather when opened. Damage can happen very quickly, so if you bring leather items, be sure to check them regularly.

MONEY

Since money makes the world go round, we wanted to share some important tips on how to manage your money from purchases to banking. Although United States dollars are accepted and even preferred at times to the local colón (₡) in Costa Rica, any foreign currency must be in very good condition or it will not be accepted. There must be no rips or missing corners, no stains or writing, and moderate wear is acceptable. However, if the bill is damaged in any way, it will be rejected.

ATM machines are available throughout Costa Rica. Most ATMs will dispense either U.S. dollars or Costa Rican colónes. Fees for these transactions are covered later in the Banking section.

Exchange Rate

The colón is the currency of Costa Rica. The exchange rate varies, but when this book was written, the rate was somewhere around 550 colónes to the United States dollar. Realizing that a single colón is worth a fraction of a penny, it can make the conversion seem like a daunting task. We will try to explain the process in a simple way to help it make sense.

When purchasing items from street vendors and small shops, they will generally use a 500 to 1 ratio, making for easier math. Using this ratio, you can take the price in colónes, double it, and then move the decimal three places to get the dollar amount. For example, if a t-shirt costs 8,000 colónes (pronounced 8 mil because mil means thousand in Spanish), you would double it (16,000) then move the decimal to get the U.S. equivalent of $16.00 (8000≈16). Converting can get confusing when dealing with larger amounts, but the same principle applies. If a house costs 175,000,000 colónes, it would be around $350,000 USD using the 500/1 ratio. The opposite conversion is relatively easy as well. For example, if we have $15 in our pocket, the equivalent is 7,500 colónes.

Of course, when using the 500/1 ratio you are losing about 9¢ per dollar depending on the exchange rate. This i s n ot too much of an issue for small purchases, such as souvenir trinkets that are under $10; however, the example of the house would cost you $318,181 if you use a ratio of 550/1, so you would save almost $32,000 by paying in colónes.

The bottom line is that whatever currency the item is listed in is usually the most cost-effective way to pay. There are fees and inconvenience to exchanging money that must be taken into consideration, so if you are planning on spending a considerable amount of time in Costa Rica, it is worth using the local currency as much as possible.

Common Costa Rican Denominations & Approximate U.S. Value.

Table 1 - Basic Currency Conversion

Coins	550/1	500/1
₡20	$.04	$.05
₡50	$.09	$.10
₡100	$.18	$.20
₡500	$.90	$1.00
Paper		
₡1000	$1.82	$2.00
₡2000	$3.64	$4.00
₡5000	$9.09	$10.00
₡10000	$18.18	$20.00

Banking

Assuming you did not plan on hiding your money under your mattress, you will most likely need the services of a bank at some point. With technological advances and internet banking, the need to have a local bank has declined. Even with these advances, it doesn't change the need of transforming the digital money into cold hard cash. We will discuss the logistics and fees associated with banking in Costa Rica both with local banks and those back in the States.

If you are planning to keep your account in the U.S. and/or are planning to make transfers to Costa Rica, you may run into issues. Many banks and especially credit unions will not make wire transfers to international banks. This can become problematic if you are going to try to buy a car or make other large purchases. If the bank or credit union does allow international transfers, they may have restrictions or charge high fees for those transactions. Remember the banking industry is highly regulated which makes international transactions increasingly difficult. Most international banks offer wire transfer services and other international banking needs that many smaller banks cannot. Unfortunately, this may require opening a new account for your Costa Rican banking needs.

Opening Accounts in Costa Rica

The options for opening an account in Costa Rica have limitations. Until recently few, if any, banks offered accounts to non-residents. Some banks, such as Banco Nacional, offer accounts to foreigners, but there are restrictions on these accounts. The restrictions could consist of a limit to the amount of money you are allowed to deposit, withdraw, transfer, or hold in the account. We have heard of restrictions of under $1,000, which could be an issue if you are trying to pay all of your expenses including rent out of one account.

Another consideration is whether or not the bank accepts PayPal transfers. This could be an issue if you are trying to accept payment for services or sales or purchase items from individuals, such as household items, recreational items, and vehicles. At this time, we are only aware of Banco Nacional being able to process PayPal transactions but have heard of other banks looking into offering this service.

For those who "live" in Costa Rica on a tourist visa and who have not applied for residency, the most common solution to overcome the banking hurdles is to form a corporation, which you may need when making large purchases. (You can find out more information on the need for opening corporations and the process in the section titled Opening a Corporation.) Using the corporation documents, you will be able to establish an account, but you will also need a letter from an accountant called Certification De Flujo Proyectado (Projected Flow Certification). This letter is the accountant's certification of where the funds for the corporation will come from and an estimated budget. The reason behind the Projected Flow Certification is that Costa Rica is working hard to establish the stability of their economy, and in order to comply with international banking regulations and tax reporting of other countries, they must verify all sources of money coming into the country.

ATMs

Similar to other countries, Costa Rican banks make their money from charging fees for their services. For transactions with foreign banks, in addition to a transaction fee, you may be required to pay an exchange fee if changing for one currency to another. When withdrawing colónes from the ATM, you may be charged a fee for the transaction, usually around $4.50 USD, and an exchange fee to exchange the dollars from your bank to the colónes of the local one, usually between 0 and 1% exchange commission, plus a flat fee of $1–$3 USD per transaction. It is advised that you check with your U.S. bank as to what fees they charge for international transactions.

Our Story — Banking

We use Charles Schwab (not an endorsement, just a fact) because they reimburse ATM fees and do not have international transaction fees. The major reason they offer these free services is that they do not have their own ATM or branch locations for banking services. You set up your account at one of their investment brokerage firms or online, and they use online resources and other banks' infrastructure to handle day-to-day operations. Some international banking institutions offer similar products where fees for international transactions are waived or at least minimal, but make sure you read the fine print to avoid a surprise when your statement comes.

Tip → *If you are planning on opening a new account, we recommend doing it as soon as possible. We had an issue when we tried to increase our daily withdrawal limit for a large purchase. We ended up needing to do a wire transfer that took extra days because our account was less than three months old and the policy didn't allow increased limits with that short of account history.*

Remember to notify your banks of your travel plans prior to leaving the country so they don't decline foreign purchases. This can save you the embarrassment at the register where lack of understanding the language may cause additional confusion about the issue.

Credit Cards

From an early age, we were cautioned about the evils that can come with the use of credit cards. What was not shared so freely were the benefits that can be accessed through their use. We have a background in finance and mortgages and have witnessed the destruction of families' financial security caused by the improper use of credit cards. If you intend to use a credit card, we cannot emphasize enough the importance of responsibility and self-control. Assuming you are able to exercise discipline and restraint, there are some very useful benefits of making purchases with credit cards, but, first, let's cover the areas of caution.

Fees

Interest charges can quickly negate any benefits of using credit cards. Make sure you understand the way interest is charged and how much you will be required to pay. Many cards offer interest-free purchases as long as the total of the purchase is paid within thirty days. Others have six months of interest-free purchases, but use caution. In most cases, these offers come with the catch that if not paid fully in six months they will charge you the interest for those six months at the start of the seventh month. Also, balance transfers are not generally included in the interest-free offer, so you will need to be able to pay the full amount or face the interest charges. If you can understand the interest-free option, this is a great way to improve your credit score with no cost to you. By keeping a low balance and paying it off regularly, you are showing that you can manage the responsibility of credit.

Other costs of using credit cards come in the form of fees. Common fees to watch out for include transaction fees, foreign transaction fees, and exchange fees to name a few. Make sure you read the fine print and understand what fees you may be liable for. There are many "travel" credit cards that offer benefits including reduced fees. These cards allow you to make international purchases without paying extra. From a fee standpoint, it is as if you were using your card back home. If you are considering using a credit card, find one that does not have fees for international purchases.

Miles

It is very likely that you will wish to return to where you came from at some point in time. The visits home are inevitable. Whether it is simply to visit family and friends, or work, a wedding, or a funeral, something will call you back. One way to minimize the cost of these visits is to use "miles" or "points." If you sign up for a credit card that offers these benefits, you will accumulate miles until you have enough to cover the cost of a travel expense.

The rate of accumulation varies between companies and can also change based on your credit history. Many cards will even offer several bonus miles if you spend a certain amount during an introductory period. It is best to get an accumulation rate of at least one mile to every dollar spent. Depending on the credit card, you may have the choice to use these miles for airfare, hotel, or car rentals. Others offer even more options for using your miles. Every time you purchase milk or fill up your car with gas, you can earn miles toward your next visit thus minimizing its expense.

Our Story — Money Management

We have a Capital One Venture One credit card that we use on an extremely regular basis. Most of our daily purchases for food, gas, and entertainment are bought using our credit card. With the exception of places that are cash only, the card is widely accepted with chip technology, and we have not had any problems using it to complete purchase transactions. Our card offers interest-free purchases if you pay within 30 days. We pay the card off monthly to avoid any interest charges. The convenience and benefits of using the card make it our primary payment source.

HOUSING

As with most areas of the world, every community has a range of housing options that vary greatly in price and amenities. You may have seen reports or read books and articles that discuss how cheap it is to live in Costa Rica. Our experience has taught us that these articles are referring to remote properties that are not located anywhere near local amenities, such as shopping, restaurants, and possibly even gas stations. These cheaper homes are what we call "tico homes" which are simple homes with basic construction (unfinished walls, metal roof, etc.) and few amenities. Hot water is rarely found in these homes. Most do not have air-conditioning and may not even have screened windows. While this could be very appealing to some people, we felt it was in our best interest to find an expat community with gringo style homes to ease our transition.

You will need to decide what amenities you *must* have. We have never liked cold showers, so hot water in the shower was a must for us. Our first home had hot water in the shower but not in any of the sinks. This forced us to change the way we cleaned and did laundry. We try to keep our costs down with limited air-conditioning so the ability to open windows for airflow was important; however, you may feel that the airflow is less important if there are no screens on the windows to keep the mosquitos out. (Once again, an issue we discovered with our first home.) These are some examples of the simple challenges you will encounter daily in your new environment when searching for a home.

Security

Costa Rica is a developing country whose economy is not strong. The average wage is under $3/hr. It is very tempting for low-income people to steal what they can't afford. Costa Rica is a fairly peaceful country, but they are known for theft. Most attempts are non-violent, yet like other countries, you will hear of a murder occasionally. We have heard that there is a tico saying of "we are thieves, not murderers." Usually, the homes that are vacant or not guarded are the targets.

Where you live will determine the amount of home security you will need. We have been fortunate that we have not yet experienced any theft attempts; however, some of our friends and neighbors have had break-ins and been robbed. Most houses and multi-unit complexes have walls or metal fences. Many homes in both city and rural locations have bars on the windows. Most multi-family units have guards.

Common sense dictates that if you are flashing your electronics and expensive items you are making yourself a target. This is where discretion can save you from being a victim. Nicer homes usually have nicer stuff in them, so obviously, they should be protected accordingly. If you are planning on exploring Costa Rica or returning home on vacation, it is advisable to find a house sitter. The simple presence of someone on the property increases the odds of your stuff being there when you get back. Use your head, and you should be able to reduce the likelihood of falling prey to thieves.

Renting a Home

Long-term rentals (one year or more) will get you better pricing than short-term. This is especially true during high season when tourism is at its peak. During this time the town experiences a large influx of vacationers creating a large demand for housing. Without a long-term lease, from November through January, you can expect to pay three to five times as much for your rental. By no later than the first part of August, you should have a signed lease covering the months of December and January. Locating property that will be available during high season will grow increasingly difficult and expensive as you approach those months.

Where do you go to find rentals? Short-term rentals can be found through sites like Airbnb and Trip Advisor. Some can be found on Craigslist as well. Be sure to read recent reviews to find out about features and issues of the property. Check the photos to ensure they are recent or ask for recent photos to be sent to you.

For long-term rentals, this is relatively difficult to do from afar. Unless you are very familiar with the area from previous visits, understanding the benefits and challenges for each property will be extremely difficult. The location of your property could make it more susceptible to flooding, infestations, or mold issues. Costa Rica does not have enforced noise ordinances. Keeping this in mind, bars, barking dogs, cars with loudspeakers, farm animals, and machinery nearby may be more than you can handle.

A local who referred us to an expat is how we found our first two homes in Costa Rica. We have also had some success using the internet to locate long-term rental property. If you are in Costa Rica, you can join multiple Facebook groups for the local area with names like (your area name) "buy and sell," "chit chat," "gringo," "expat," "garage sale," etc. Remember that these groups have people from all over with various opinions, and bear in mind the risks of social media. Another source is Craigslist. If you are local, you can drive by the location to ensure it is in the same condition as when the photos were taken. You would be surprised how quickly the climate can deteriorate an unmaintained home.

Rental management companies work with renters and rentees. As a renter, these companies will show you the properties they manage and meet whatever criteria you may have. There is not a centralized database for multiple companies, so you have to check with each one individually. Some companies have a niche market that they focus on, whereas others have a broad spectrum of options. Depending on your criteria, you will need to choose which approach best suits your needs.

As a rentee looking for someone to manage your rental, the rental management companies offer management packages that can include: booking, access, rent collection, maintenance, cleaning, gardening/pool, and security services. The rate for management depends on the services you require. These services can greatly simplify the management of a rental and in some cases may be required by the homeowners association.

RECOMMENDATION

For rental services, we have worked with a couple different property management companies. We can tell you from experience that RPM Vacation Rentals offers the best management services in Tamarindo. From courteous and knowledgeable bilingual staff to the rapid response of service calls, RPM takes care of business. We recommend their services to both renters and rentees.

Home Rental Cost

As you can imagine, several factors determine the cost of rentals in Costa Rica. Besides the varying space, quality, and upkeep, things like proximity to the beach, proximity to shopping/tourism, swimming pools, common spaces, and security will have a great impact on the amount you pay. Most apartment or condominium projects have common areas with a gardener, security personnel, and cleaning services included. If you choose a house in a remote location, you will probably pay less in rent but may have to forgo or absorb the cost of those types of services.

In the northern coastal Guanacaste area, you can expect to pay $650–$1,500 for a furnished North American style two-bedroom home. Three bedroom units start around $800. The lower end will be further from town and the beach and will have few amenities if any. You may be asking yourself, "Hey, wait a minute, didn't we just see a place for rent for $300 per month?" Yes, there are properties in that price range, but what you will get is a tico home with no hot water, no air-conditioning, no pool, and worn out furniture (if there is any provided at all). Our assumption is that you want your transition to be successful, and although you may be able to "rough it" as a tico, your family may not. The North American style homes should provide a smoother adjustment to the culture shock you may experience.

We would like to note that dishwashers are not common in Costa Rica. The homes that have them usually don't use them due to electricity cost and the hard water causing regular repairs. We have visited many friends who have broken dishwashers and very few who have them use them. Garbage disposals are much of the same story.

Our Story — Housing

For our first home in Costa Rica, we found a one bedroom apartment in Langosta for $700 per month including utilities. This was a multi-unit building with four units that shared a pool and laundry machines. The property was walled in and was supposed to have a weekly gardener; although much of the time we were there, no one tended to the property. The pool was cleaned weekly, and residents were responsible to clean the common areas themselves. One of the major issues with this property was water shortages.

On several occasions, we went multiple days without water. The property had a small, shared water tank that was adequate for the number of users as long as it filled on a regular basis. Our first year had a long drought with water restrictions that prevented the tank from filling often. (See our section on Water in the Utilities chapter for more information about dealing with these issues.) We only stayed at this home a couple months to reduce our costs from the hotel while we searched for alternatives with more room for our family.

Our second home was a two-bedroom apartment that was designed to sleep ten people for $1,000 per month with the utilities included. Both rooms had permanent bunk beds constructed of one full and three twin beds sleeping five each. It was designed for short-term surf groups to be able to pack many people into one home. Because we were having trouble securing long-term housing close to the beach we talked to the owners and were able to convince them to lease it long term. The downside was that we had to move out during the peak weeks of high season because the owners were not willing to give up the $10,000 per week that they made during that time. Since finding alternative housing during those high times was very challenging, we decided to find another permanent home.

The reason utilities were included in our first two properties is due to them only having one meter for the multi-unit building. The property management wanted to split the bill evenly between all of the units, but we were able to negotiate the contract so that we paid a flat fee with utilities included. You will learn more about utility costs in the coming sections.

With a great amount of research, we were recently able to locate an apartment in Tamarindo approximately three-quarters of a mile up a hill from the beach for $1,000 USD/month (utilities not included). Although some may be willing to make the fifteen-minute walk to the beach, we find we would rather drive and spend our time on the beach especially when we decide to take our surfboards or beach equipment like a cooler and chairs. The apartment complex is relatively small with less than ten units and a beautiful and decent sized pool with a barbeque grill included in the gazebo. We have a gardener during the day and a night guard. The rent includes weekly cleaning service, which we could have more frequently if we paid extra.

The building is fairly modern and is decently maintained with standard appliances, hot water in all of the sinks, and air-conditioning in all of the rooms. We do not have a view of the ocean or a valley but are fortunate that there are some vacant lots surrounding the property with many trees for the birds, iguanas, and howler monkeys to visit. We feel this is a great blessing. For some, waking up to the sound of birds and monkeys is an annoyance. For us, grabbing a cup of coffee and watching the world come to life is one of the things that inspires us to get out of bed.

Buying a Home

First, we must recommend **living** (not just visiting) for at least a year in the town of Costa Rica where you are considering relocating. It would be even better to rent the home you are considering purchasing for that year. If you are looking at building a new home, we recommend watching the property for the year to see what happens to it during both the rainy season and the dry season since some properties experience severe flooding during rainy seasons. The property may have a great view during dry season when the trees are bare, but be completely obscured by leaves and vegetation as soon as the rain starts. You may think you have found a paradise with the wildlife you have dreamed of only to find out that those animals migrate through and are not there nine months out of the year. These are just a few circumstances that have happened to people we have met.

Once you have committed to buying your home, we recommend using an official real estate agent with an office. There are no licensing laws for real estate agents in Costa Rica. When you tell someone you wish to buy a property, they immediately tell you that they can help you and proceed to show you every property of every one of their family members. Everything is for sale for the right price, and everyone becomes an agent to sell it to you.

All property is transferred through attorneys. This includes homes, vehicles, boats, businesses, etc. You will need an attorney for multiple things in Costa Rica so we would recommend interviewing a couple to determine which you feel most comfortable with as you may need them for more than just this transaction.

If you are considering purchasing a unit in a multi-unit complex, make sure you research everything you can about the property and who has control and authority over what. Are the utilities separate or do multiple units use the same meters? What about common areas? Who's responsible to maintain them? How are the expenses for electricity and water of the common areas divided? These questions become increasingly important if there are vacation rentals in your complex. Vacationers do not use restraint when it comes to utility use. With the beach nearby and the need for bug spray, it is not uncommon for some to take several showers a day. Vacationers often leave the air conditioners running the entire time of their visit. If utilities are divided, you could be in for a shock when paying more than your share during high season.

Our current rental is one unit of a complex that has individual owners for each of its six units. Each unit pays a large HOA fee, $525 per month, to cover utilities, maintenance, and security of all common areas including the pool and rancho area. We came to find out that the homeowners do not own the pool. It was never included in the development purchase and the person who owned the land before the complex was built still owns the pool. So, one of the best assets of the property could be sold to a separate party and/or use could be denied. There are various situations similar to this that can reduce the appeal and value of the property.

Our Story — Searching for Property

Our first week in the country, we knew we had to find a place to live fast. The internet had filled us with the hope of finding an extremely cheap home by talking to the locals. Although we expected to rent, we were open to buying if the right opportunity arose since we had resources to do so.

We connected with a couple of local guys we met on the beach who claimed to be agents. We didn't find it unusual that they were always barefoot because they were surfers. These gentlemen asked if we had a car because they did not. Being ready for adventure and having no idea what to expect, we agreed to rent a car so they could show us around. They showed us several properties of a wide range of quality. At every home, we seemed to pick up another person until we had one of the property's owners following us in his car to his relatives' house where we continued our parade picking up additional passengers until that car was full too.

The homes we were shown were primarily "tico homes" with no air-conditioning and in fairly poor condition. Remember we were looking for a steal, right? Most homes had families in them that had no idea we were coming. The families would just go about their business as strangers wandered through their messy homes. As former real estate agents, this was not what we expected from our first real estate experience. When we finished viewing the last home, the driver of the other car asked for some money for gas since he had led us to a few of the homes. Being fresh in the country we had no idea if this was the custom or what, so we gave them a couple thousand colónes (around four dollars) and thanked them for their help.

We have since viewed property with a couple different agents from offices. These showings did not resemble our first day of viewing property at all. They were very professional and much like you would expect from the United States; however, these showings were not near as eye-opening as our first.

RECOMMENDATION

For professional service that rivals what you would receive in the States we recommend agent Stacey Watson at ReMax Ocean Surf & Sun. She has lived in Tamarindo for over 20 years and gained experience building The Monte Perla condos. From cabina to castle, she can handle the purchase.

UTILITIES

If you have a Costa Rican bank account, you can pay your utilities online. Another option is to pay your utilities at most large grocery stores and banks. We rarely go to the bank since the grocery store has an ATM and that is where we pay the bills anyway. We withdraw what we need and pay at the checkout register (caja in Spanish). All utilities must be paid in cash. They do not accept debit cards or credit cards for these payments unless you pay online. You will need to be able to supply the service provider, account number, and name on the account.

Many homes have propane stoves and/or barbeque grills, and some even have propane clothes dryers. Property managers and realtors can provide the phone number for the local gas company which will deliver and install the propane. After numerous house explosions, the government passed regulations requiring the gas company to perform all tank swaps.

Electric and water utilities must be in the owner's name. If you are renting, you will be paying the owner's account. Other utilities such as internet, cable, and telephone can be put in your name. You will need to consult the property management company to find out how they have utilities set up for your property and to get the account numbers needed to make payments.

Our Story — Utilities

Our first few homes in Costa Rica had free Wi-Fi included in the rent. What was not clear is that the internet service was a shared connection with the other units in the building. This became problematic for trying to stream on multiple televisions and for gaming. If Wi-Fi or internet is included, we recommend you take your laptop and tablets with you to inspect potential homes and check the connection and speed of the internet service. Bear in mind the time of day and how many neighbors are home when you test the connection.

At our current condo, we started with paying the cable/internet through the property management company, but they changed their policies and now require long-term tenants to transfer the cable/internet services into the tenants' names. At this point, we were allowed to choose whomever we wanted to provide the service. After research, we decided to continue with Tigostar because our results showed them to be the most reliable and cost-effective option in the area.

Utility Costs

Depending on where you live, you may have different

usage rates for electricity. (Fortunately, we do not live in one of those areas.) Some areas charge a premium for usage during daytime hours. This means that if you run your air-conditioning during the day your bill will be extremely high. Another consideration is that the housekeeper comes during the day to take care of laundry and run the dishwasher (if you are fortunate enough to have one). These appliances use a lot of electricity, which would be cheaper if it took place at night. Also, if you live in the central valley or mountainous areas, you can expect to have less usage overall than areas along the northern coast where it is hotter and you use more electricity and water. If you are trying to move to Costa Rica on a budget, this Utility chapter may have the most impact on your ability to afford to live here full time.

Electricity

This will most likely be your biggest expense and have the greatest impact on your budget. Remember, some regions have additional rate changes and peak hours. In our region we pay $0.13/kWh for usage up to 200 kWh and $0.19/kWh for any usage over 200 kWh. Our bill usually runs about $250/month. We use two A/C units at night and watch a lot of television with gaming systems and computers. We do not have a dishwasher but do use a washer and dryer for our clothes. We also have an instant hot water system that uses additional electricity.

Major appliances, like laundry machines and ovens, are common in expat homes but most ticos do not have them with the exception of the refrigerator. Many ticos burn wood on cinder-block-constructed grills to prepare their meals, and they use pilas (large concrete or tile sinks) for laundry and dirty jobs. Many homes do not have hot water or it is limited to only the shower. All these factors can have a major impact on monthly electricity expenses.

Power Outages

This is a fitting time to discuss power outages. Electrical outages are a very common occurrence in Costa Rica. Most power lines are overhead and not buried due to the high water table. This means strong storms with high winds or enough rain to cause mudslides can take out power lines. Due to continual erosion, some trees are not stable and will fall across the lines on calm days as well. Where we live, one set of lines comes into town and through it to the next town of Langosta. If the lines go down or a transformer blows outside of town, it can take out the power to multiple towns. The electric company is working on installing another set of lines, but at this point, we have only one source for our power.

We are not sure why but power outages occur mostly at night, possibly because storms are strongest then. Most outages only last a half hour or less; however, we have been without power for up to eight hours. We lose power an average of once every couple weeks but more frequently during the rainy season.

We do have "flickers" in the power where it shuts off for a few seconds to a minute and then comes back on. These are much more frequent than outages. We can have a couple of "flickers" in one day but generally experience them less than ten times a week. If your stove is electric, this turns off the oven leaving the meal uncooked until the oven is turned back on and the timer reset. We try to use a phone timer so we know how much cooking time is left. And of course, the internet modem resets during "flickers" so we have a brief loss of service that usually occurs at the climax of our Netflix show or while trying to upload large files.

If your work is computer-based or relies on electricity, we recommend investing in a battery backup. This may not keep you connected to the internet, but it will give you some time to complete whatever you are working on and maintain productivity until power is restored. With our children in online school, we make sure they download the materials needed for their assignments ahead of time so they can work offline if we lose internet connectivity.

Tip → *Since power outages are common, place flashlights and candles throughout your home for safety. Know where the spare batteries are—it is extremely frustrating searching for batteries in the dark. Be proactive and download some entertainment while you have service. Netflix and Amazon Prime allow you to download some of their media for offline viewing. If you are a reader, having a few books downloaded to your Kindle or e-reader can be a great blessing. E-readers are generally better than books in the dark until the e-reader goes dead. Once the electronics' batteries have died, you will want to have a deck of cards, some board games, and a book with a reading light around to pass the time. On occa-*

sion, our family opts for the unplugged entertainment of games and looks forward to the next storm for the rematch.

Water

Water cost is a bit difficult for us to pin down. Some factors that impact the cost are whether you have a pool, if you water your landscape, and how the cleaning staff uses the water. It is not uncommon to see the staff use the hose to clean off patios, etc., even during drought season where water usage should be kept to a minimum. Water outages and rationing is another impact on the monthly cost. That being said, we average around $50 per month in water usage. Our current condo has one water meter for all of the units, and the usage is then divided evenly. Since the $50 we mentioned is an average, understand that we pay more when the units are filled due to higher usage and less when it is just our family on the property.

Be aware that during the dry season in Costa Rica, water shortages happen, and many municipalities impose water restrictions and ration the water. Often the town will turn off the water during midday hours to minimize usage. Most Costa Rican properties use a tank system where the tank fills whenever the water is available. Depending on the size of your tank, you may not even notice that the water was turned off.

Our Story — Water

Our previous home in Langosta had a small water tank

that was shared by four units. Langosta imposes water restrictions during much of the dry season. At one point, our tank did not fill for fifteen days. The house across the street had a trickle of water, but the pressure was so low that the slight elevation to our property kept our tank from getting any water. We had to use the pool for bathing and the pool water to flush the toilets. We purchased several large bottles of water for cooking and what little cleaning we had to do. Those fifteen days were our longest period of time without water, but during the year that we stayed in Langosta, we went without water for more than three days on five separate occasions. We were very blessed to have friends that allowed us to use their laundry machines and take showers. The laundry service in town charged on a per kilo basis, and our one large load would cost $25. (This included them washing, drying, and folding the load.) Our budget also had to absorb eating out more frequently since we had limited water for cooking and cleaning of pots, pans, and dishes.

Propane

Propane is currently close in price to the U.S. If you are choosing your appliances, you may want to consider the power outages. If you have a propane stove/oven, it will continue to work when the power goes out. If you are trying to minimize expenses, a smaller tico propane oven will save you over the large U.S.-style oven. In our first home, we cooked for four people on a full-size propane stove/oven and had to replace the propane once a month. At our second home, we cooked for the same four people on a smaller tico propane stove/oven and replaced the propane every three months. Both stoves used the same size tanks. This shows the difference the size of the appliance makes on usage. Regardless of size, given the option, we would elect to have propane cooking appliances due to price and function.

Cable and Internet

Current promotions show that 8MB internet and 100+ channels of digital cable costs ₡29,000 or around $50 per month. Faster internet and larger channel packages are available. Of the cost of the service, the majority is for the internet, not the television. Our TV service costs us about $4. The TV channels include both Spanish and English channels, and not all of the channels offer the English option. (You need to be familiar with the SAP feature of your television to change the language settings.) Our package has about half of the channels with an English option.

We primarily watch Netflix, but it is nice to catch the news from the States and watch some sports. We receive U.S. stations from Florida so our "local" news is whatever is happening in Florida. Our package includes HBO, Cinemax, Fox, FX, AMC, TLC, TNT, NBC, CBS, ABC, E, WB, A&E, Discovery, Disney, CNN, and several others. If you want, you can purchase the standard sports packages to catch all the games. (Check with the local provider for availability and price.) Very few channels are missing compared to what we had available to us in the States. Although these channels were available to us when we lived in the U.S., we canceled our cable and satellite service due to the price. The bundle internet and cable packages here have been more affordable allowing us to enjoy the addition of cable television.

When considering your internet needs, keep in mind some of these factors. Building construction in Costa Rica includes a lot of concrete and rebar. Although a Wi-Fi signal can pass through these materials, the signal is definitely weakened by them. We have had trouble getting Wi-Fi signal to some of our bedrooms where the signal was blocked by multiple walls. We linked an additional router to extend the signal range, and some of our friends have used signal boosters to address the same type of issues.

If you are planning on using the internet for work or school, be aware that the speed of your service will probably decrease during peak seasons such as Christmas and Samana Santa (Holy week of Easter). As we mentioned in the Electricity section, power outages will affect your internet service as well. If your work is dependent on reliable internet, you may have issues during both peak season and power outages. We recommend downloading any necessary materials on a regular basis so you can maintain productivity during the outages.

A separate option from standard cable internet is to use a mobile data hotspot device or use your cell phone as a hotspot. We have some single friends who choose this option so they can take their internet wherever they go. This would not work for us because if one of us takes the hotspot the rest are without internet service. Check the Claro website for rates and options. (http://www.claro.cr/portal/cr/pc/personas/internet/)

Our Story — Cable and Internet

We previously mentioned the need to transfer the cable and internet services into our name. To do this, we called the local number (where they did not have an English representative) and were informed we needed to go to the main office in Santa Cruz, the capital of our region. We made the forty-five-minute drive to Santa Cruz where a very friendly representative who spoke almost no English told us we needed an appointment with the local salesperson. With our limited Spanish, pointing, and some Google Translate, she helped us pick our package and scheduled an appointment for the local sales person to visit our house.

We are not completely convinced that the trip to Santa Cruz was necessary and believe that *had* we been able to speak Spanish we may have been able to schedule the sales visit over the phone. Regardless, two sales representatives that spoke minimal English came to our home and ordered our service to be installed and established in our name. The install happened three days later by a technician that also spoke almost no English. Since then we have had no issues with the service and pay our own bill at the grocery store.

Telephone

Landlines are available throughout much of Costa Rica, but almost everyone uses cellular phones. Part of the reason for this is the number of landlines is limited, which means there may not be one available. To setup landline service, you must have a Cedula (Costa Rican ID card issued to residents).

One of our biggest savings has been on our cell phone bills. We have found that cell phone service is very affordable in Costa Rica. Monthly contract service is available for around $60–80 per month if you have a Cedula. Our family, like most expats, use the prepaid option. We average around $5–10 per month per phone. This is largely due to the use of web-based apps like Facebook Messenger, What's App, and Instagram as our primary form of communication. We turn off our data when not in use and connect to Wi-Fi whenever possible. (Wi-Fi is available in most restaurants, bars, and many businesses although you may need to ask for the password.)

If you are planning on bringing a cellular phone, make sure it is an unlocked GSM phone. CDMA phones will not work here. When you change the SIM, you'll automatically be able to tether and make a hotspot. When you tether your phone, you allow other devices to share your internet connection. That service is free with a prepaid Kolbi plan unlike in the United States. (As soon as you return to the States, you can use a prepaid gringo SIM card, but you will be locked out of tethering. The U.S. companies want you to pay a monthly fee for that service.)

Two brands of SIM cards are available in Costa Rica—Kolbi and Movistar. Kolbi offers the most geographical coverage while Movistar has several dead zones throughout the country but works well in San Jose. Save or write down the APN settings for Kolbi Costa Rica from the internet. They should look something like this:

Figure 1 - Phone Settings

APN	kolbi3g
User name	
Password	
PDP Type	IP
Auth Type	PAP
MCC	712
MNC	01
Dial number	*99#
Carrier	Kolbi
Android APN	kolbi3g
APN type	default,supl,dun
Auth type	PAP
Carrier[2]	Multimedia
Android APN[2]	kolbi3g
MMSC[2]	http://msice

When you land in Costa Rica, don't waste your money in the airport. Buy a SIM card from a mini super (convenience store) or pharmacy. Pop in the SIM, enter the puk code from the card that the SIM comes in, and follow the prompts to enter the pin, etc. Then enter the settings you downloaded into your phone. If you are unfamiliar with this process, you can watch a YouTube video with instructions. Just search for: "how to change APN settings on Android (iPhone)." Once you enter the settings, you will be able to make calls and use data.

We brought our Verizon Samsung Galaxy phones from the States, and they worked just fine on the local network. Before we left, we paid all remaining balances for the contracts since Verizon would not unlock the phones until our contract was paid in full. If you bought your phone through your cellular provider, you will need to check with them about their policy of unlocking phones.

Phones that are locked are still able to connect to Wi-Fi the same as they would in the U.S. If you don't make telephone calls but simply communicate through web-based apps, you may not need phone service at all. Your limitation would be that you would need to be connected to Wi-Fi service so communication would be kept to within reach of the Wi-Fi signal. This approach also applies to tablets. When our friends visit, they don't purchase phone cards but simply use web-based apps to share their experiences with their friends and family back home.

Tip → If you are planning a trip and are expecting to use your phone for navigation, we recommend logging into your app while connected to Wi-Fi prior to leaving to reduce mobile data charges. On Waze and other similar apps, this will download the trips entire map reducing the amount of data used and allowing for more accurate directions while out of cell range. The voice direction and nearly all other features work even while offline. Keep in mind that if you are out of range or have your mobile data turned off you will not get updates about delays, police sightings, and hazards.

In addition, you may want to consider downloading media such as music, videos, or movies to your devices while connected to Wi-Fi for offline entertainment as well. We download our favorite Spotify playlists and a few Netflix movies or shows regularly to be ready for both road trips and power outages.

TRANSPORTATION

When using public transportation (buses and taxi cabs), keep the following tips in mind. With the exception of the tour shuttle services, very few of the drivers speak English. It is best to know the name of your destination and possibly some nearby landmarks, such as stores, restaurants, or hotels, to ensure the driver knows where you want to go. If you ask for a ride to the beach, there may be multiple entrances so knowing what is nearby is very helpful. Having small bills or exact change is advised as this helps speed up getting on and off the bus and ensures you don't receive incorrect change back from cab drivers.

Considering renting a car or even buying one? Your valid U.S. state issued drivers license allows you to operate personal vehicles in Costa Rica. There are restrictions on operating commercial vehicles or machinery. (Contact COSEVI (the Costa Rican equivalent of the DMV) for license restrictions on specific vehicles.) When driving, always carry both your valid driver's license and a photocopy of your passport including the visa stamp with the date on it. If you are stopped by a transito (traffic cop), you will be required to produce these documents, along with the proof of current Marchamo and RETIVE which will be discussed further in this chapter. Usually the window stickers for Marchamo and RITEVE are sufficient and they won't ask for the documents, but it is a good idea to keep copies in the glove box.

It is not uncommon to see both random and standard traffic stops. There are a couple places on the road to Peñas Blancas for border crossings where transitos often place a checkpoint stop. Other times the transitos will pull up to a spot and park on the side of the road where they will flag random cars to stop. The primary purposes for these stops are usually to enforce visa regulations, ensure valid drivers licenses, and ticket colectivos, unofficial taxi's which we discuss in the Taxi section. Unless the transito waves at you, you simply need to slow down but not stop. If you are waved down, use the etiquette you *should* use at a traffic stop in the States and you will not have a problem. Just like most places on the planet, if you show respect, you will be treated with respect back. The officer may or may not speak English. Usually if they examine your documents and don't see an issue with them being expired, etc., they will let you go on your way without even finding someone to translate.

At one stop, we happened to have our passports with us because we were heading to the airport. When Steve produced his passport with his license, he was instructed by the transito to only have a photocopy of the passport and visa stamp and to leave the passport back at the hotel. He assumed we were tourists. His advice was sound though; your passport should be kept in a safe place and not carried around with you. We cannot tell you how many stories we hear of people having to request a replacement from the embassy because theirs was stolen.

Tip → *For directions, we recommend downloading the Waze app. In our experience, Google Maps was not as accurate as Waze. Many ticos use Waze and update it fairly regularly with transito sightings, accidents, and objects on the road (usually fallen trees, mudslides, or cattle). This will also assist you through the cities with one-way traffic where reading signs may be difficult. Nikki especially enjoys the "Boy Band" option for the audible directions.*

Road Conditions

Where to begin? The quality of road conditions is about as diverse as the climates in Costa Rica. Along our travels, we have experienced large freeway type roads, such as the Pan-American Highway which is a divided highway with multiple lanes of traffic, as well as dirt roads that are completely rutted out, barely able to fit a small car, and underwater in some places. Most areas you can get around perfectly fine with a compact car but off the main roads you may find yourself in need of a four-wheel drive (4WD) vehicle.

If you are planning on taking a drive to an area you are unfamiliar with, we recommend doing some research first and keeping your expectations for road conditions low. We try to check our Waze app and ask various Facebook groups about road conditions whenever we feel adventurous to explore new places or if we need to be somewhere at a specific time. With the possibility of traffic stops, downed trees, road work, and poor road conditions, a simple trip to the next town can end up taking most of the day. Although traffic is free-flowing most days, it is when you need to be at the airport or at a special meeting that these issues tend to arise. If you plan ahead to leave early and use technology to check road conditions, you can increase your chances of being where you need to be on time.

Tip → *It is always a good idea to keep a small emergency kit in your vehicle when traveling outside your local area. We would recommend a plastic tub with a small first-aid kit, a couple bottles of water (for you or your radiator), a flashlight, basic tools (knife, screwdrivers, pliers, duct tape, superglue, zip-ties, etc.), rain gear, and a towel or blanket. If there is an accident or your car breaks down, these items can be very valuable to you.*

National Roads

The majority of national roads, those owned and maintained by the country, are in good condition. Many are paved with lines painted on them and relatively few potholes or damage. Some are multi-lane, such as the Pan-American Highway, while others are simple single lane bi-directional roads. Because the country is maintaining these roads, they generally stay in good condition and are worked on often. This has been a frustration for us as we watch what are perfectly good roads being resurfaced instead of the resources being used to fix the roads that are barely drivable.

It took us a long time to understand that the issue lies in who is responsible for the upkeep of each road. Overall, the national roads are usually the smoothest and best maintained.

Municipal Roads

These roads are the responsibility of either a town or province to create and maintain. We find the greatest disparity in the quality of these roads. Most municipalities have very limited resources to create and maintain their roads, which is quite evident once you begin driving on them. A road to the south of where we live starts out paved but because of heavy rains has giant potholes for the first two kilometers (or just over a mile). The road continues and turns into a dirt road that is often smoother due to recent grading than the paved section with all the damage. Most towns will try to pave or frequently grade the main roads in and out of town but will give minimal attention to the side streets and less traveled ones. Occasionally businesses will pay to grade or pave sections of roads leading up to their businesses. As long as the business is successful, the road stays in good condition, but if it is left to the municipality to maintain, they may have other priorities.

Back Roads

Backroads can be anything from a beach road that weaves out of the jungle, onto the beach, and back to a dirt path leading to pavement to a high-quality private road, bought and maintained by a homeowner. Some back roads are private and should be marked as such, where others are public roads with minimal traffic and minimal upkeep. We have found some extremely beautiful places by venturing down a back road leading into the jungle. Sometimes these roads can be scary and even 4WD is not enough. It is not uncommon for cars to drive off cliffs or roll off embankments.

A major issue with these back roads is rainwater. **Do not drive through water especially if it is flowing.** It is surprising how deep some holes can get, and it only takes a second to get stuck. Many streams and rivers have roads running through them. During the dry season, the road is clear, and you would think nothing of it. With a little rain, it does not take much of a current to lose traction and push a car downstream.

A few years ago, a group of our friends was following cars trying to get out of a neighborhood when the rain started. A few cars had crossed a low spot in the road where a stream was building as it flowed across the road. The water was rising quickly. When the small truck in front of our friends' vehicle started to cross the stream, the water lifted the truck. The truck lost traction and was quickly washed downstream where it lodged against a tree. The episode happened quickly, and it could have been avoided if the driver would have exercised caution.

Bus

There are several different options for buses. Some are more direct while others make frequent stops. Most buses are

fairly recent models and in good condition, much like the Grey-
hound buses in the United States. If you are planning on traveling
to a town that is a considerable distance, the Ticabus or Empresa
Alfaro are good choices. For more local travel, there are a few
options, such as Tralapa Bus Company, La Pampa Bus Company,
or Transporte Cabo Velas. From Tamarindo to Huacas (approximately 10 km or 6 miles), the cost is ₡500. The Transporte Cabo
Velas will charge you incrementally if you choose to get off before
you reach Huacas, but the La Pampa buses will charge you the full
rate regardless of where you depart the bus. In addition, friends
have reported times where the La Pampa drivers were rude, and
the buses didn't stop when they tried to wave them down. We have
not heard of that issue with the Transporte Cabo Velas bus; they
seem to always stop to pick us up.

Colectivos

The most affordable option is probably the colectivos.
Colectivos are drivers without a taxi license that drive around in
sedans picking up passengers. They pick up multiple passengers
along the way and charge each person individually. Usually, they
will not pick up more people at one time than they have seats for
due to fear of being caught by the police. However, we have seen
some colectivos with multiple people, usually children, on people's laps. In one trip from point A to point B, you may ride with
ten other people who were picked up and dropped off before you

arrived at point B. A standard fare for the colectivos is ₡500 from Tamarindo to Villa Real or ₡1000 to Huacas per person.

When colectivos see someone standing on the side of the road or walking, they will flash their lights, honk, or wave out the window to signify that they are a colectivo. If you don't want to wait for a colectivo to pass, you can wave to sedans as they approach, and before you know it, one will pull over for you. If you're trying to survive on a tight budget and don't mind riding with multiple strangers, colectivos may be for you.

Taxi

Regular taxis are available that you can call, wave down, or find at the taxi station. It is a good idea to ask the rate before you get in. The drivers have fairly standard rates, but some try to make a little extra. Below is a list of common destinations and an approximate cost to give you a point of reference.

Figure 2 - Taxi Fares

Tamarindo to Langosta: ₡1000–₡1500

Tamarindo to Villa Real: ₡2000–₡2500

Tamarindo to Huacas: ₡7,500–₡10,000

Tamarindo to Flamingo: ₡12,500–₡15000

Tamarindo to Brasilito/Conchal: ₡12,500

Tamarindo to Playa Grande: ₡12,500

Tour/Shuttle Vans

If you want to take tours to see the amazing sights of Costa Rica or need transportation to or from the airport, tour/shuttle vans are a good option. The drivers almost always speak English and some vans even include free Wi-Fi. Some of the drivers are very knowledgeable about the culture as well as the history. When we took a tour in the Rincon De La Vieja region, we chose to ride in the tour van. The driver began sharing information as we left Tamarindo, and we learned about the various crops, landscape, and cultures along the way. As we climbed in altitude, the driver talked to us about the coffee plantations and different forests and plant life that changed as we passed from one microclimate to another. The driver was like our own personal tour guide on a driving tour to our destination.

In addition, we have used the shuttle vans for airport transportation. Our first experience with these services was upon our arrival to Costa Rica. As we walked out the glass doors of the air-conditioned customs area and through the wall of hot humid air, we were directed outside to an area where people wait for their passengers. This area is for commercial drivers, as well as friends and family waiting for incoming passengers. It can be a bit chaotic with drivers shouting out the names of people they are there to pick up. Our hotel had arranged the shuttle service when we made our reservation, and a kind smile and a sign with our names on it greeted us. Easily enough, the driver helped load our luggage and took us to our destination.

When we use the shuttle to take us to the airport, we have always arrived on time and never had an issue. The drivers pick us up at our home, and there is plenty of room for our luggage. Depending on the number of passengers, the shuttle has the potential of being cheaper than driving yourself to the airport. This is especially true if you are planning on paying to park your car while you are gone; however, if you are willing to risk leaving your car unattended, you are allowed to park at the airport for free. We have left our car at the airport without issue.

Tour/shuttle vans are a great option for groups and special events. The vans are spacious, clean, and modern, complete with air-conditioning. They allow large groups to travel together, and you don't have to worry about getting lost or spending your vacation focusing on the road. If you have a large family or are traveling with friends, these vans may be a great option.

Tip → *If you are a small group or solo passenger, there are ways to utilize these services. There are Facebook groups where you can post your travel dates and see if others are interested in using the vans with you. If you call the shuttle service directly, they will often reserve a spot for you until they have enough others to form the minimum group size, usually four people.*

Gasoline

Should you choose to forgo the public transportation option you will need to use the services of the bombas (Spanish for "pumps"). There are a few major differences in the way gasoline is handled here in Costa Rica.

First, it is controlled by the government. As such the price of gas is the same at every gas station in the country. You don't need to shop around for a good price, which is a good thing since there are not gas stations on every corner. You can find mini supers everywhere but not gas. In fact, Tamarindo does not have a single gas station. We have to drive 8.4 km (5 miles) and almost two towns away to fill our tank. The next closest is a nice forty-five-minute drive of farm and forest land winding 36 km (22 miles) to the city of Santa Cruz.

Second, in contrast to the self-service standard of U.S. gas stations, you don't exit your car in Costa Rica. You simply pull up to the pump and ask the attendant to "llenar" or fill your tank. If you ask, the attendant will check your tires and wash your windshield. When done, he will take your payment through the window and return with a receipt. (See our Prices section for gasoline prices.) Unless you need some snacks or the restroom, you simply stay in the car until finished and drive off.

Tip → *Pay attention to the sale total on the pump. A common problem in many parts of Costa Rica is skimming an extra mil or two (around $2–$4) by running your card for slightly over the actual cost. On one occasion I caught an attendant trying this approach. When I pointed to the pump showing an amount 1,000 colónes less than the receipt, he simply pulled the cash out of the register and handed it to me. No harm, no foul, I was on my way.*

Renting a Car

Costa Rica has several companies offering rental cars. Some international chains, such as Hertz, Budget, Economy, etc., are available as well as local companies. We have learned that although several companies advertise rental car options for under $50 per day and as low as $10 per day, these rates do not include all fees and insurance required by Costa Rica. Although our credit card offers car rental insurance, it is not sufficient to meet what is required by the nation so the insurance offered through the rental company is generally best. Unless you choose a monthly rental, you can expect to pay $80 or more per day for a small car rental. If you are quoted a very reasonable rate, do not be surprised if you are charged additional fees at checkout.

Another consideration when renting a car is that with some companies and for certain vehicles you are not allowed to drive on some roads. Some companies will not cover damages incurred on roads other than the main streets of towns and connecting highways. If your intention is to get off the beaten path and visit a remote beach or jungle area, you may be risking a lot. Make sure you ask for any restrictions on where you are able to take the vehicle and read the small print.

Leaving items in rental cars is not recommended. This includes your luggage, phones, sunglasses, backpacks, etc. Do not be obvious when placing your stuff in the trunk. We have seen a video of men watching people load their possessions into the trunk, and as soon as the people leave, the thieves break into the trunk and take everything. This is very common, especially in the cities and at the beach.

Tip → *Make sure you have sufficient room on your credit card for your rental. Most companies require a deposit that is a hold on the account similar to hotels, which can take several days to be released. This fee will reduce the funds available and can impact your ability to make other purchases on your travels.*

Our Story — Car Rental

The first time we rented a car we were not very concerned with the price because we really needed the ability to travel where we wanted when we wanted. This was a straightforward transaction where we paid the high rental price of $89 per day with the insurance through the rental company.

The second time we shopped around to try to find the cheapest option. We've heard many stories reporting the challenges of renting cars including price changes, the cars not showing up as scheduled, and the rental companies not assisting stranded drivers.

Since one of our biggest concerns was price, we searched the internet for the option with the better reviews. None of the reviews were great so we decided to book with Budget. Their website advertised that we could rent a car for $15.95 per day. We were going to waive their insurance and simply use the insurance offered by our credit card to keep the price down. The website said the price included all taxes and required fees. When we arrived to collect our car, it was not at the airport where the website said to collect it. Instead, we had to drive back to the center of town to the office where no one was on duty. The sign on the door showing hours reported that the office should be open, so we called, and eventually someone showed up to assist us.

We asked about the price, and the worker confirmed that it would only be the reported $15.95 and that we could use our credit card insurance. We handed him our credit card for payment. After processing the rental including payment in the system, he presented us with a receipt showing a rate of $120 per day. Obviously, this was not what we agreed to. When we challenged him on the amount and reminded him that we had asked up front about the rate, he reported that the $15.95 was their fee and the remainder was the taxes and insurance that the Costa Rican government requires. He offered a smaller car and fewer options and was able to reduce the amount to $90 per day, but that was still more than we wanted to spend. At this point, we canceled the rental, which took three days to return to our credit card, and resumed our search for a more affordable option.

Buying a Car

If you have given public transportation a try and it just doesn't suit you, or if you need the freedom or usefulness of your own vehicle, you may want to search for reliable transportation. However, depending on where you choose to settle, you may not have access to car lots. There are a few car lots outside of the cities of San Jose, including its surrounding suburbs, and Liberia. If you are looking for a brand new car, you will either need to travel to one of these locations or have a new automobile shipped in. Since Costa Rica does not manufacture any automobiles, you are going to pay import tax on any vehicle transported into the country. In addition, cars hold their value longer as long as they are well maintained. For these reasons, purchasing a vehicle in Costa Rica can be pricey.

When we first moved, we were not sure if we were going to buy a car. We had heard great things about the bus system, and we had been told that cars cost a lot of money. We came to find out that they do cost a lot of money. We never thought we would be in our 40s, spending $10,000 on a fifteen-year-old car, and feeling like we got a great deal, but that is what happened.

After being in the country for three weeks, we were finding it hard to look at properties, bring home groceries, and travel to different offices and agencies to establish ourselves. Our food bill was outrageous because we were shopping at the mini super store down the street from our home, where we had a limited choice of items at a high price. If we were to take the buses, we had to leave very early for appointments, and the taxis were adding up quickly. Since we had made the choice that we were going to work online jobs and travel all over the country, it only made sense to buy a car.

We searched the internet for used cars in the area since we did not have means to travel far to pick one up. Because we like to explore and believe that part of our experience is getting out and seeing as much of the country as possible, we decided we needed a 4WD vehicle. On Craigslist we found a Jeep Cherokee with a lift kit and surf rack that not only met our needs but looked pretty sweet as well. The Jeep was in Playa Coco, about 45 minutes away. We contacted the owner, an Italian gentleman that spoke mediocre English and broken Spanish, and once he determined we were serious about buying the Jeep, he drove it down for us to look at.

We test drove the Jeep and everything seemed in good order, so we offered to purchase it. We made sure that the Marchamo and RITEVE were paid up to date. We also wanted to make sure we had a couple months before we had to take care of anything big. At this point, we had to work out the payment logistics. We did not have a Costa Rican bank account at that time, and as we discussed in the Money chapter, our account in the States would not let us withdraw enough for the purchase through the ATM. We were told we could go into a local bank, and they would be able to complete the withdrawal.

We took a $60 taxi ride to Playa Coco to meet the seller at the bank. At the bank, we ran into issues. Speaking almost no Spanish, we struggled to explain what we were trying to do and finally got the answers we needed. We discovered that although the withdrawal was possible, the bank was going to charge over $1,000 in international transfer fees. It only took us about two hours in the bank to get to this point where it seemed like the deal was going to fall apart.

The solution we came up with was to request a wire transfer of the money directly to the seller's account. The transaction was going to take five days to process completely. We processed the payment on our end and provided a printout of the wire transfer request showing the account it was being sent to. From there we went to a local attorney to complete the property transfer.

The attorney was able to include the payment arrangement in the paperwork. We agreed we would not take possession of the Jeep until the payment was fully processed. We struggled a lot with this risk, and if it were not for the attorney including it in the contract, we would not have been willing to leave without the Jeep in our possession. Actually, Nikki was not at all okay with the arrangement and had her "I told you so" card in her hand ready to throw it at Steve when everything unraveled. The seller gave us a ride home, and we agreed to meet up in a couple days once everything processed.

Thankfully, things didn't unravel. The money transferred as planned a few days later with less than a $50 wire transfer fee, and we took another $60 cab ride to go pick up the Jeep. The doubt didn't end there for Nikki as she spent the car ride home waiting for the wheels to fall off. We wish we could say that everything about the transaction was just as it was presented, but we did discover that the air conditioner had a leak and stopped working within a week of purchase. Even with this issue, we have been pleased overall with the purchase and have seen several areas of Costa Rica thanks to our Jeep.

Marchamo

As in the United States, there are legal requirements on

vehicles using the public roads in Costa Rica. Marchamo is similar to paying a yearly license plate tax in the U.S. It includes the taxes, registration, and basic liability insurance required for each vehicle. Payment of the Marchamo is due between November 1st to December 31st of each year. There are relatively high penalties for late payment and high fines if stopped by a transito and the Marchamo is expired.

Beginning in November of each year, you can find out the amount owed for Marchamo on the INS website Marchamo section or on the Costa Rican banks' websites. The amount for Marchamo is determined by the year, make, and model of the car. To give you an idea on how much Marchamo costs, our 2001 Jeep Cherokee's Marchamo for 2016 cost ₡102,594 or about $186. Remember, that cost is for a fifteen-year-old vehicle; vehicles with a higher market value will cost more.

If there are any outstanding traffic or parking tickets associated with the car, the system will report those, and payment of all amounts due will be required in order to renew the registration. Payment and registration can be completed at Costa Rican banks using the plate number or directly to a MOPT Ministry of Transit location. You will not be able to renew or pay a Marchamo unless you can show proof that the vehicle has an up-to-date RITEVE (RTV) receipt showing that the vehicle has passed its yearly inspection.

By simply using the license plate number, anyone is allowed to pay for a Marchamo even if the vehicle is not registered in his or her name.

Once the Marchamo is paid, a new official circulation card is issued and should be kept with the other vehicle forms. This card also comes with a sticker that is required to be posted on the passenger corner of the car's windshield.

RITEVE or RTV

RITEVE is a vehicle inspection that is required each year for all street legal vehicles including trucks, cars, motorcycles, scooters, four-wheelers, etc. This inspection primarily focuses on the safety features of the vehicle, such as lights, seatbelts, tires, horns, and general operation of the vehicle. To complete the inspection, you must make an appointment at the RTV office. You can call one of the offices to schedule the inspection, or you can schedule it online at the RTV official website by entering a telephone number and the vehicle's license plate number.

You can normally get an appointment within two weeks. When the appointment is scheduled, you will be provided with a confirmation date and time, along with a list of things to present. The RTV test costs 10,920 colónes (approximately $20) for cars and 7,195 colónes (approximately $13) for motorcycles.

Figure 3 - RTV Documents Needed

Documentation needed at the inspection:

- Title deed to the vehicle (Titulo de propiedad)
- Registration card (Tarjeta de circulación)
- Some form of official ID (passport, drivers license, etc.)

Although the RITEVE is similar to emissions testing in the States, it is a more intensive inspection than a simple emissions test. For most people, RTV is a stressful scary place to wait and hope and cross their fingers that their vehicle will pass the first time. Even brand new cars fresh off the trucks have been known to fail on the first try. Sometimes cars seem to operate fine with no known issues, but their alignment is off or the hand brake is too weak and needs to be adjusted, so the vehicle doesn't pass. Simple items like over or under full oil or tire pressure can cause a car to fail as well. Although they may be a mess cosmetically, vehicles need to have *everything* in working order including seat belts, windshield wipers, horns, electric windows, etc.

Many people make the mistake of going to RTV without doing a simple inspection at home first. Some issues can be easily corrected and failures avoided if the owner takes the time complete their own inspection. RTV is not only testing for CO_2 levels, they also test brakes, shocks, lights, tread on tires, and more. We had to have fenders made for our Jeep since the off-road tires stuck out beyond them. This is, of course, a safety concern, especially in the rainy season when tires throw water and mud at other vehicles. Our friends have a vehicle that has removable third-row seats. They did not have the back seats in the car for the inspection and failed because the seatbelts were still there so the seats needed to be too.

If a vehicle does not pass the RTV test the first time, the inspection will have to be repeated as many times as it takes until all of the issues have been corrected. This can become a very expensive and time-consuming process requiring multiple trips. It is best to allow the test to be completed even after a failure is found in order to locate all issues and potential faults. This may reduce the number of re-inspections required to get the vehicle to pass by allowing you to address all of the issues at once.

Once the vehicle has passed the inspection, the driver will receive a RTV receipt that needs to be kept in the glove box. A sticker will also be issued and needs to be placed on the windshield near the Marchamo sticker on the passenger side. This sticker indicates the month the car will be required to complete its next inspection. The RTV inspection month never changes as it is based on the license plate number. It is a good idea to start the inspection process a month before the inspection is due to ensure it is completed before expiration. This is especially true for a car that is new to you since you may not be familiar with its issues.

Each year RTV laws get more stringent in an effort to increase safety and decrease emissions. To stay apprised of these changes and keep informed, visit the RTV website for any changes to requirements and faults.

We do not take our vehicle to inspection ourselves. Our mechanic offers a RITEVE service where they will inspect the vehicle themselves prior to taking it to the office. Our Jeep has a light bar on top, which is technically illegal. Our mechanic removes the lights prior to inspection and replaces them when it is done. They take care of the entire process, so we don't have to worry about it. The mechanic schedules the appointment, which seems easier for them since they take several cars for inspection and have developed relationships with the workers at the office. They take the vehicle to the inspection, watch it take place, and discuss the failures with the RTV worker. If possible, they will correct the issue immediately. Since we speak limited Spanish and are not very car savvy, it would be challenging for us to understand and be able to correct all of the problems discovered by the inspectors. With our mechanic's experience, we have been able to avoid costly and inconvenient re-inspections. The mechanic charges $100 which we initially thought was a bit much, but with the ease, reduced stress, and time savings, we have decided the $100 is well worth it.

Insuring a Car

Costa Rica requires basic insurance that is paid through the Marchamo, which every vehicle is subject to. The basic insurance is in some ways similar to liability insurance that is required in most of the United States.

Tip → *This insurance only covers injury and death, not property. If you are in an accident and at fault, you will need to have additional insurance to cover damages to any vehicles involved or you will be required to pay for these damages out of pocket. If you are not at fault and the other driver does not have additional insurance or the means to pay for the damages, additional insurance may be the only way to avoid paying for repairs to your vehicle out of your own pocket.*

Figure 4 - Obligatory Insurance Coverage

Obligatory Insurance for Motor Vehicles covers:

As established in article 64 of the Transit Law 9078:

"The Obligatory Insurance of Motor Vehicles covers the injury and death of people who are victims of a traffic accident, whether or not there is subjective liability of the driver.

"Likewise, the injury or death occurred in a civil liability accident, arising from the possession, use or maintenance of the vehicle.

"In the latter case, this responsibility must be established through established procedures and before the competent courts." (Frequently Asked Questions, 2017)

You can visit The Istituto Nacional De Seguros (INS) office or speak to an agent in your area to ask about additional insurance options. Although most people do not purchase additional insurance, we felt it would be best to protect ourselves and our assets in the event of an accident since automobiles are expensive and our budget does not support replacing one. Keep in mind that since most people don't have insurance, the person at fault may not be able to afford to fix your vehicle. Also, if you're at fault, you may not be able to cover the damages to multiple other vehicles. We currently pay ₡229,485 ($417) per year, which we feel is worth the cost for the peace of mind.

Our foremost warning about accidents is do not leave the scene until either a transito officer or Red Cross representative clears you to leave. If you leave prior to being cleared, no insurance will cover your liability, property, or medical. It may take some time and traffic may back up for a long distance, but don't feel uncomfortable — waiting is the requirement. We have passed several accidents including some that have had traffic stopped for over an hour without moving.

Car Repair and Breakdowns

If you haven't picked up on it by now, the Costa Rican environment is hard on things. The sea air and the rains combined with the temperatures and rutted roads can wreak havoc on your auto. If you purchase a car, you will want to find a good mechanic to keep it running smoothly. You may need to work with more than one mechanic before finding one that you trust, but we have found that mechanics in this country can be very resourceful. We tried a few mechanics and have come to love and trust our friends at OMC Tamarindo.

In our experience, mechanic labor is cheap in Costa Rica. Most times, when we have taken our car in to be worked on, we have paid less than $20 in labor. Parts, on the other hand, are a much different story. Because everything is imported, parts are expensive and/or hard to find. This is where the resourcefulness of the mechanic comes in. If the part is not available, the mechanics often find a work-around or fabricate what is needed.

We have an aftermarket lift on our Jeep that requires bushings that we could not find anywhere in Costa Rica. Our mechanic tried to order them based off of their exact measurements, but since they were aftermarket and a much different size than the factory ones, he was not able to find any. He recommended we have Teflon bushings made like the ones on the Argentinian race trucks. He said they would be lifetime bushings and not wear out like the rubber ones. The fabricated bushings were cheaper than getting aftermarket ones shipped and have held up beautifully.

One of the benefits of our mechanic, and many others here, is that they respond to breakdowns if we're in the area. As we have mentioned, we enjoy exploring and have a tendency to get bored, load up in the car, and find a random road to follow and see where it goes. This has put us in some challenging positions where we have had to ask our mechanics to come rescue us.

Our Story — Car Breakdowns

The first time we broke down, we had been out exploring about 30 km (approximately 20 miles) away from home during the dry season. We were following a dirt road up over a hill when we first smelled smoke. It is not uncommon to smell people burning their trash or yard waste, so we thought nothing of it. As we came to the top of the hill, the Jeep started cutting out. We pulled off the road into a clearing, and as soon as we opened the door, the smell of gas filled the air. We looked under the car and saw gas spraying onto the ground. About this time, we realized that we hadn't smelled someone burning their trash but rather a wildfire that was spreading across the side of the hill.

We immediately jumped back in the Jeep to try and make

our way out of there. We bounced and raced down the rough dirt path back to the main road. Nervously, we watched as the smoke got closer and closer. Remember, *we were leaking gas!* Knowing we needed help with the Jeep, we tried to call the mechanic but did not have cell service. We turned down the main dirt road and managed to reach the paved highway. With the fuel needle dropping, we chugged past flames and firefighters a few yards up the hill from our car until we reached the end of our tank of gas about a quarter mile past the spreading fire.

Back in cell range, we called our mechanic Mario. His wife Lucia, who always answers the phone, asked if we could send our Waze location. We sent our location, and Mario and Lucia came to our rescue. Mario was able to make the repairs to the fuel line with the parts he had brought with him. Since the nearest gas station was about 15 miles away, he found a small store in someone's home that unofficially sold him some gas in a plastic Coca-Cola bottle. And we went on our way away from the fire.

Our second breakdown included a broken belt that got jammed in a pulley. Of course, it had to be the serpentine belt. Because we were about 45 minutes from Tamarindo, we were too far away for our mechanic to come to our rescue. However, he helped us call a tow truck to bring the Jeep back to Tamarindo. We sat by the side of the road and waited for the truck. After about two hours, a flatbed rolled up and hauled our Jeep to the mechanic's.

Sounds easy enough, right? Now re-read that last paragraph and imagine being stranded in a small Costa Rican village where no one speaks English. This is an example of how normal stressful situations can be even more challenging when you are out of your element and don't speak the language.

Although the tow truck that handled this incident was just like the ones back in the States, it was one of very few that we have seen in this country. In most cases, cars are pulled behind other cars usually with rope but sometimes with straps or chains. We have assisted a few individuals ourselves, even towing our buddy's motorcycle to the next town.

RECOMMENDATION

We first worked with OMC Tamarindo in their old location which was a tiny lot, crammed with cars, and only an open-air tin-covered structure big enough to park three cars under. They have since moved locations and grown to include lifts, an actual office, and other amenities. The owners have made quite a few repairs and upgrades to our Jeep. We have had good experiences with OMC Tamarindo and feel it is one of the best mechanic shops around.

Tip → *While we are on the topic, we should mention that we often bring car parts back with us when we return from visiting Colorado. We have brought everything from chip keys to rain guards. We regularly bring headlights back as they seem to dim quickly here. Some items you can find here, but once again, the price is an issue.*

SHOPPING

Costa Rica manufactures very few products and imports the vast majority. With this in mind, it is understandable that the cost of most goods is going to be high due to basic supply and demand principles. Costa Rica's population is 4.8 million (roughly the same as the state of Oregon), which is only 1.5% of the 321.4 million people of the United States. The consumer pool is much smaller, so businesses must select only those items they know will sell. Because of these factors and others, the diversity of product options is less than in the United States.

Our experience has taught us to be open to trying other brands, styles, etc., and that if we find something we especially like, to purchase it because it may not be there the next time. This includes everything from furniture to dishwashing soap. We have had to change our thinking to stop saying "This is way more expensive than in the States" because it doesn't matter what it costs in the U.S. Our present reality is that we are in Costa Rica so the value or cost of an item is based on our current economy. This mindset is how we decide what is worth throwing in our suitcases, what we can live without, and what we are willing to pay more for than we did in the past.

For example, our children did not eat peanut butter during the first nine months after our arrival. In the States, peanut butter was a *major* staple, and they consumed it at a rate of about a large jar a week. Although peanut butter is available at most stores, it has a very high markup making it a specialty item for us. Several months passed until we had a visitor bring some with them. This experience helped us appreciate the small things in life like a peanut butter and jelly sandwich.

While we didn't do much online shopping when we lived in the U.S., it has become a big form of shopping for us now. Since our time is limited when we visit the States, we use online shopping to purchase many products we need ahead of time and have them shipped to our family members in the States. This saves us spending our vacation time shopping and allows us to spend more time relaxing. We bring the items back with us after our visit or have people visiting us bring whatever items they have room for.

We don't have things shipped to us in Costa Rica because it costs too much for taxes and import fees and things might not show up. The Costa Rican Embassy in Washington DC reports current maximum values of merchandise you can bring into the country before being required to pay taxes on those items.

Since we visit the U.S. about once a year, we have to think about a whole year of shopping ahead of time. When we leave Costa Rica, we cradle our empty suitcases inside of one another to bring back to the States and fill them up as full as we can. While we have found some decent stores that carry many different things: underwear, socks, shirts, etc., we have found that there are limited styles and sizes. Our kids have become very select in what they own since they only get one suitcase a year.

Another area of learning that has opened a new world for our family is food. Most fruits and vegetables common to Costa Rica are a stark contrast to what we were used to in the United States. Even things like watermelon and pineapple taste considerably different. The proteins—meat, chicken, pork, and fish—have a different taste as well. Costa Rica has less GMO crops, and most animals are free range. These along with other food production practices affect the taste.

There seems to be a stronger emphasis on fresh foods like bread and produce than processed packaged foods probably due in part to the importance placed on health in the country. With all these differences, our family has enjoyed trying new meals and unusual fruits and vegetables. Many food options look very strange or unappetizing but are quite delicious. Although Costa Rica is not known for great cuisine, we have certainly broadened our tastes and have enjoyed more fresh fruit and vegetables than we used to.

Tip → *If you need to get something from the States ASAP and you don't have an option of friends or family coming for a visit, there are Facebook groups that can assist you in finding travelers who are willing to carry items to you in Costa Rica for a small fee. You can join these groups and offer to bring things for people as* *well. Search Facebook for groups with the keywords "mule to Costa Rica." Remember if you don't know exactly what you are transporting and where it has been, you may be putting yourself at risk.*

Mini Super

Throughout Costa Rica, "mini super" shops are like convenience stores. These shops can be part of people's homes or in commercial complexes. The further away from tourist areas, the more often they are part of a family's porch rather than their own entity. Most of the mini supers have eggs, milk, drinks, liquor, and dry goods (bread, beans, rice, cereal, etc.). You can likely find some cheese and/or baked goods, such as empanadas and sweet breads, made by local families as well. As in other countries, you pay for the convenience of the location of these shops so the prices are considerably higher than the larger mercados (markets).

Grocery Store/Mercado

In cities and tourist areas, large grocery stores not only stock produce, deli, and bakery items but also stock a lot of the same products you would find in the U.S. (You can get your bag of Cheetos to go with your Betty Crocker cake mix.) Grocery stores in Costa Rica offer the staples you need and may also provide some comforts of home, albeit at a price. (Check the section on Prices to see what items may be expensive or difficult to find.)

Some stores offer sale days where they place several items on sale every week. Each store has something different to offer, and you may pay a bit more for items in a cleaner and more modern store.

Location is also a major factor in price. If the mercado is in the center of town within walking distance to many people, the prices may be slightly higher.

If you have done some research and heard about the Wal-Marts in Costa Rica, you should throttle your expectations. Yes, there are Wal-Marts in a couple of large cities, but the stores are not nearly as large nor do they have the variety or quality of products compared to the stores in the United States. You may be able to find some items cheaper at Wal-Mart than in smaller towns, but often the savings and selection are not worth the time and gas money.

Carnicería

Although you can purchase meat and poultry at the grocery stores and some mini supers, another option is to buy from the local butcher shop called a carnicería in Spanish. We prefer the meat from Centro De Carnes Villa Mar, the carnicería in the nearby village of Villa Real. The Costa Rican meat does not contain the coloring, preservatives, or steroids found in most of the meat in the United States. Because it lacks these additives, the meat has a slightly different taste that may take some getting used to. The meat is generally leaner, so it doesn't cook quite the same as what we were accustomed to. (This became very evident when we tried making hamburgers!) We find ourselves eating more chicken than beef or pork simply because it tastes great.

Ferias and Fruit Stands

For produce, there is the option of the ferias and fruit stands. Ferias are similar to farmers markets where various farmers and vendors sell produce and goods, whereas, fruit stands are generally a single private owner selling items from their own farm. We have a fruit stand in nearby Villa Real that is open every day, but most ferias are only open once or twice a week. Tamarindo has a feria located off the beach that is open on Saturday mornings where local farmers and merchants bring produce and goods to sell. There are several fruit stands both in towns and along the roads throughout the area. We choose to get our produce from the fruit stand called Come Fruta in Villa Real, as it seems to be fresh good quality at a low price.

Pickup Truck Produce

When the farmers or families with fruit trees harvest, they often load the back of a pickup with their produce and park on the side of the road in the middle of town. Many of our friends have commented that the best watermelon and pineapple they have ever eaten was off a pickup truck in Costa Rica. This is often a great way to purchase unique produce at a good price. Our family recommends you try some Mamon Chinos and Maracuyá. Don't be scared of the spiky appearance or slimy texture, just open your mouth and let your taste buds enjoy the tropical goodness.

Household Goods

For things like laundry baskets, kitchen items, plastic containers, etc., stores like Maxi Pali or Mundo Magico are in the larger towns. The nearest one to Tamarindo would be in Santa Cruz about 45 minutes away. Many towns have smaller stores simply known as "plastic stores." The prices are usually slightly higher than the larger stores but what you save in gas when purchasing a few items makes up for it.

For appliances, furniture, fans, etc., there are Coopeguanacaste and Gallo stores in many towns throughout the area. Remember these items will cost more than in the States, so you may want to fit small appliances like blenders and juicers in your luggage.

Prices

Prices on items in Costa Rica are going to be in local currency (Colónes – ₡) and use the metric unit of measure. For those coming from the U.S., this means a double conversion of a unit of measure and currency. Here are a few formulas to help calculate the conversions.

Items in Kilos vs. Pounds

Produce & deli products are sold in kilograms (2.2 lbs. per kilo).

Formula ₡ per Kilo to $ per Lbs.
Equation 1 - Kilograms per Colónes to Pounds per Dollar

$$\frac{₡\text{Price}}{\text{kilograms}} * \frac{1(\text{kilo})}{2.2(\text{pounds})} * \frac{\$1}{₡550}$$

Example: One kilo of chicken breast costs ₡6,425. If we place that price in the equation we get the following:

$$\frac{₡6425}{1(\text{kilo})} * \frac{1(\text{kilo})}{2.2(\text{pounds})} * \frac{\$1}{₡550} * \frac{₡6425}{1210}$$

Chicken breast costs $5.31 per pound.

Items in Liters vs. Gallons

Liquid is sold in liters (3.79 liters per gallon or .264 gallons per liter)

Formula ₡ per L to $ per Gal.
Equation 2 - Liters per Colónes to Gallons per Dollar

$$\frac{₡\text{Price}}{\text{liters}} * \frac{1(\text{liters})}{.264(\text{gallons})} * \frac{\$1}{₡550}$$

Example: One liter of unleaded gasoline costs ₡700. If we place that price in the equation we get the following:

$$\frac{\text{¢700}}{1(\text{liters})} * \frac{1(\text{liters})}{.264(\text{gallons})} * \frac{\$1}{\text{¢550}} * \frac{\text{¢700}}{145.2}$$

Unleaded gasoline costs $4.82 per gallon.

*Exchange rate of ¢550=$1, you will need to update with the current exchange rate for accuracy. (See the section on Exchange Rate.)

Price Charts

Although prices for goods are constantly changing, we thought it might be helpful to include a snapshot of the current prices in the area. Of course, by the time anyone actually gets here, the market may have fluctuated and the charts on the following pages won't be completely accurate, but hopefully, they will give you a point of reference.

Table 2 - Prices

Item	Protein		Dollars $
	Colónes ₡		
Hamburger 90%	CRC 7,045.00	per kilo	$5.82 per pound
Steak Sirloin	CRC 9,235.00	per kilo	$7.63 per pound
Steak T-Bone	CRC 16,525.00	per kilo	$13.66 per pound
Chicken Breast	CRC 6,425.00	per kilo	$5.31 per pound
Chicken Legs	CRC 3,865.00	per kilo	$3.19 per pound
Pork Steak	CRC 13,615.00	per kilo	$11.25 per pound
Ham	CRC 13,315.00	per kilo	$11.00 per pound
Bacon	CRC 10,850.00	per kilo	$8.97 per pound
Red Snapper	CRC 7,005.00	per kilo	$5.79 per pound
Talapia	CRC 10,200.00	per kilo	$8.43 per pound
Shrimp	CRC 32,630.00	per kilo	$26.97 per pound

Produce

Item	Colónes ₡		Dollars $	
Apples	CRC 4,095.00	per kilo	$3.38	per pound
Avocado	CRC 4,830.00	per kilo	$3.99	per pound
Carrots	CRC 815.00	per kilo	$0.67	per pound
Celery	CRC 2,155.00	per kilo	$1.78	per pound
Cucumber	CRC 935.00	per kilo	$0.77	per pound
Lettuce	CRC 645.00	per head	$1.17	per head
Lime/Lemon	CRC 2,836.00	per kilo	$2.34	per pound
Onion	CRC 1,226.00	per kilo	$1.01	per pound
Oranges (local)	CRC 3,850.00	per kilo	$3.18	per pound
Passion fruit (Marycoya or Granadilla)	CRC 2,000.00	per kilo	$1.65	per pound
Peppers (similar to bell)	CRC 2,785.00	per kilo	$2.30	per pound
Pineapple	CRC 1,470.00	per kilo	$1.21	per pound
Potato	CRC 1,443.00	per kilo	$1.19	per pound
Tomato	CRC 2,415.00	per kilo	$2.00	per pound

Drinks

Item	Colónes ₡		Dollars $	
Milk	CRC 1,950.00	per gallon	$3.55	per gallon
Orange Juice	CRC 760.00	per liter	$2.62	per 1/2 gallon
Coffee	CRC 5.50	per gram	$4.54	per pound
Tea - Lipton Yellow Label 200g	CRC 3,570.00	per box	$6.49	per box
Coca-Cola	CRC 0.64	per milliliter	$1.16	per liter
Jack Daniels Whiskey	CRC 30.90	per milliliter	$42.14	per 750 milliliter
Smirnoff Vodka	CRC 9.05	per milliliter	$12.34	per 750 milliliter
Bacardi	CRC 7.25	per milliliter	$9.89	per 750 milliliter
Jose Cuervo Tequila	CRC 16.93	per milliliter	$23.09	per 750 milliliter
Cacique Guaro (domestic sugar cane liquor)	CRC 5.25	per milliliter	$7.16	per 750 milliliter
Beer - Imperial (domestic)	CRC 4,250.00	per 6-pack	$7.73	6-pack

Staples

Item	Colónes ₡		Dollars $	
Baking Powder	CRC 6.95	per gram	$0.36	per ounce
Baking Soda	CRC 2.00	per gram	$0.10	per ounce
Butter	CRC 6.25	per gram	$0.32	per ounce
Bread (Fresh)	CRC 1,000.00	per loaf	$1.82	per loaf
Bread (Sandwich)	CRC 1,500.00	per loaf	$2.73	per loaf
Cheese - Slices	CRC 15.57	per gram	$0.80	per ounce
Cheese - Shredded	CRC 9.14	per gram	$0.47	per ounce
Flour	CRC 0.69	per gram	$0.57	per pound
Milk	CRC 1,950.00	per gallon	$3.55	per gallon
Sugar	CRC 0.65	per gram	$0.54	per pound
Peanut Butter - Jiffy 16 oz.	CRC 3,195.00	per container	$5.81	per container

Junk food

Item	Colónes ₡	Dollars $
Lays Potato Chips 15 oz. Bag	CRC 4,950.00 per bag	$9.00 per bag
Doritos 10 oz.	CRC 2,505.00 per bag	$4.55 per bag
Frosting Betty Crocker	CRC 3,480.00 per container	$6.33 per container
Cake Mix	CRC 3,250.00 per box	$5.91 per box
Oreos	CRC 1,935.00 per box	$3.52 per box
Ice Cream	CRC 4.98 per gram	$2.40 per pint
Snickers Candy Bar	CRC 675.00 per bar	$1.23 per bar
Pringles large can	CRC 1,395.00 per can	$2.54 per can
Hershey's Chocolate Syrup 24 oz.	CRC 2,425.00 per bottle	$4.41 per bottle
Lucky Charms 326g	CRC 3,950.00 per box	$7.18 per box
Special K 13.4oz	CRC 2,795.00 per box	$5.08 per box

Other frequently purchased items

Item	Colónes ₡	Dollars $
Gasoline (Unleaded)	CRC 700.00 per liter	$4.82 per gal
Laundry Soap (liquid)	CRC 1.67 per milliliter	$11.49 per gal
Toilet Paper	CRC 8,555.00 per 18 rolls	$15.55 per 18 rolls
Dish Soap (liquid)	CRC 1,965.00 per 750 milliliter	$3.57 per 750 milliliter

Hard-to-Find or Expensive Products

It would be impossible to list every item that is difficult or impossible to find in Costa Rica. We have included a wide spectrum of categories that we have discovered to be difficult to locate or to cost considerably more in Costa Rica. Obviously, this list is in no way conclusive, but it should provide a glimpse into expensive and hard-to-find items in the Guanacaste area.

Table 3 - Expensive & Hard-to-find Items

Art Supplies $?	Kitchen Appliances $*
Athletic Equipment $*	Linens $*
Band-Aids $	Musical Instruments $*
Beauty Products $*	Over-the-counter Medication $*
Bug spray $	Peanut butter $
Car parts $*	Shoes $*
Electronics $*	Sunscreen $
Hygiene Products $*	

$ These items are considerably higher priced. You can expect to pay at least 20% more than you would in the United States. In some cases, you might pay 300–400 times as much.

?   Most items can be found in San Jose. For the most part, few stores in the Guanacaste area, if any, will carry these items, and if so, options will be limited.

*   You may be able to find these items but only in a certain brand, style, quality, or genre.

HEALTH CARE

One of the deciding factors of where in the world we would relocate was access to quality health care. As is the case with many families, we have some rather major health concerns that could require ongoing treatment. We needed to ensure that we would not need to return to the United States frequently for care. We were willing to make the trip back for annual checkups to keep our records updated, etc., but we did not want the required frequency to be more than once a year. We have confirmed what our research told us—Costa Rica has very high-quality health care that in some ways surpasses our treatment experience in the US.

Emergency Services

911 is the emergency telephone number in Costa Rica. Knowing how to call for help was a major concern once we arrived in the country. Just because someone dials 911 does not mean the response will be "immediate." It could take hours for the assistance

to arrive depending on the nature of the incident, if or who is on duty, and if they are responding to another emergency.

Medical Emergencies

For a medical emergency, the ambulance may not be what you are expecting. Some are fairly well stocked with first-aid supplies and equipment while others contain less than a complete first-aid kit. Different municipalities have different budgets and resources for these services. Even if the rig is stocked, there may only be a driver and not someone to treat or stabilize the patient in transport. There are a few private ambulance services around the country, but they are fairly sparse.

For medical emergencies, it is quite common for friends or locals to simply load the patient into a car and drive them to the nearest clinic or hospital. Often the patient will receive faster treatment than waiting for an ambulance.

Medical

It is important to note that we have paid out of pocket for medical care through private providers. Our experiences with medical care have been every bit as good if not better than what we received in the United States. We have had surgical procedures as well as routine checkups, all of which were on par with our doctors back in Colorado.

Two of the most common conditions we've needed treatment for here are pink eye and ear infections. Both of these conditions can be handled by the pharmacist, which is different than in the States; however, some pharmacists may recommend you see a doctor. Because our daughter has had multiple ear infections, we are able to simply ask the pharmacist for the antibiotic drops, and he will issue them. If the drops prove ineffective, the pharmacist will issue the oral antibiotics as well. The pink eye episodes have been much of the same with the pharmacist issuing the necessary antibiotics. Many pharmacies have doctors and exam rooms in them and others have doctors very close by. If a doctor visit is required for a medical issue, the initial exam is usually around $50 USD.

While our medical experiences have been excellent, we have friends who have used the Caja (free government care) who experienced very poor treatment. One friend was in a motorcycle accident and reported it was the worst treatment he'd ever experienced. After several minutes of trying respectfully, he had to throw his urinal (important to note that it was empty) to get the nurse's attention only for her to begrudgingly and half-heartedly clean his feet that were covered in filth from the accident. Others have reported having their broken bones improperly reset.

We have other friends who have expressed a much different experience with the government care after surgery and other medical treatments. The bedside manner was professional, and the procedures have produced great results. They did not report any mistreatment or poor experiences.

Our conclusion is that, much like the United States, people have mixed feelings about the care they receive from government facilities. Fewer complaints come from private care. If you want to hedge your bet on being pleased with the service, you may wish to consider private options.

RECOMMENDATION

Through the experience of various treatments, we make the following recommendations for these specific types of care:

Standard Medicine and 24-hour Emergency Clinic — The amount of equipment and capabilities of the Beachside Clinic in Huacas surpass most others in the area. The entire staff is friendly and welcoming. The receptionist and several doctors are bilingual. For overall care, this is a great place.

Homeopathic and Standard Medicine — For a more personal touch, we would recommend Amada Robles at Tamarindo Wellness Center. She offers standard services for things like ear infections, common colds, etc. In addition, she works with her patients to develop wellness plans which may include medication, vitamin treatments, diet, exercise, and alternative medicine methods.

Cosmetic Treatments and Surgery — The Beauty Clinic in Huacas is a professional office with current treatment methods and equipment. The quality, skill, and service provided by Surgeon Eduardo Villa Lobos is on par with the best, and he is only getting better. Dr. Villa Lobos went above and beyond in regards to personal treatment and follow-up care.

Insurance

One of the major concerns when it comes to health care is the cost. What we have found is that there are many ways to address health care costs. You can purchase international insurance, some hospitals do private insurance, and if you are applying for residency, you will be able to receive the government insurance, Caja. (A residency application can take years, and the requirements are hard to meet, so we don't recommend planning on receiving Caja.)

We have found working with the local doctors is a great way to save money. Some will do follow ups for free. If you are someone who needs regular blood work or tests, talk to your local clinic or doctor as many of them will work with you on prices. Often price-breaks and rebates are limited to "cash only" payments. It's not unusual for doctors to make home visits for no additional fee. We have had a few doctors come to our home to see a sick person for the same price that an office call would cost.

International Insurance

One way to approach the cost of health care is by purchasing international insurance. Many different insurance companies out there offer international insurance. You can choose big names like Blue Cross Blue Shield or International Care Wea. Most of these companies have online representatives that will assist you, which is helpful because you can review all of the options and apply via the internet plus the representatives speak English. Many people research and establish their policy before they leave the States. For us, locating international health insurance was fairly easy since multiple companies offered plans.

One option in Costa Rica is to use INS (Instituto Nacional De Seguro) or Costa Rica's National Institute of Insurance. INS offers international insurance that is not only effective in Costa Rica but throughout the world. This is the same company we purchased our elective auto insurance from, and we planned on taking care of our health insurance at the same time that we did our auto insurance. We quickly ran into a problem because no one could speak English in the office. We were informed they had an English representative, but he was on vacation. We felt the intricacies of insurance policies were something we needed to be able to understand in English so we took the info and contacted them through email. If you are not bilingual, we would recommend setting up an appointment before you head to the office.

Rates for international insurance vary based on co-pays, deductibles, and caps. We have been quoted rates for a family of three in 2017 ranging anywhere from $2,060 to $4,099 per year with a $500 deductible. You will need to decide how much insurance you feel comfortable with for your specific health needs.

Tip → *Watch out for caps; most international insurance have caps just like insurance in the States. A tragic accident or a sudden illness can cost a lot of money in a short period of time.*

Insurance through Hospitals

Some of the hospitals in San Jose offer private insurance, and we did something similar with the local doctors who charge $50–$60 per visit. Our insurance coverage doesn't cover hospital visits, only the local emergency clinic where they are able to do x-rays, stitches, and blood work.

We have a couple of family members who need routine blood work for monitoring. We pay out of pocket for this service, and it costs about $200. This cost includes the doctor's analysis and having it sent to our doctor in the States. This same blood work in the States would run about $550 out of pocket.

Traveling Home for Treatment

Since the Affordable Care Act requires American citizens to carry insurance in the United States at this moment, another option is to travel back to the United States for care. If you do not have the need for regular medical visits or if the visits have considerable time between them, you can often wait for treatment until you return home on vacation. This method allows you to continue to work with your current doctors who know your history. Scheduling your medical visits to coincide with your 90-day border crossings can also help reduce additional travel costs.

Paying Out of Pocket

One of the downfalls to traveling without international insurance is a sudden illness or an accident. Not having insurance is always a risk because you could be stuck with a big bill; however, keep in mind that Costa Rican medical care doesn't cost near as much as American care. We have heard many stories where people have been able to make cash payments to the hospital for a week of ICU care that cost less than a month of international insurance premiums.

Costa Rica Insurance (Caja)

While this might be an option in the long run, it probably won't be an option at first. In order to qualify for this insurance, you have to be a resident. When you become a resident, you will be required to pay into the government insurance allowing you access to the free 100% covered insurance. Bear in mind that this coverage does not cover private providers or elective procedures.

Dental

We have had quite a bit of dental work done since we have arrived. In addition to checkups and basic fillings, we have had broken crowns replaced and a root canal completed. The root canal came with an abscess that required antibiotics and cleaning out. While replacing Steve's crown, the dentist informed him that the technique used on his broken two-year-old crown had been discontinued here decades ago because new techniques showed better results in durability. Steve has had no issues with the new crown.

We have experienced some of the most painless and highest quality service in dental care in Costa Rica.

We do not have insurance so all of our dental treatment was paid out of pocket. Below is a breakdown of the cost of our treatments. Some charges were in colónes and others in dollars. For conversion please see our Exchange Rate section.

Table 4 - Dental Charges

Cleaning	25000 colónes
Filling	18000 colónes
Filling and X-ray	20000 colónes
Root Canal	$162
Porcelain Crown	$400

RECOMMENDATION

We have used a couple different clinics, all with good service, and have found DRA. Silvia Duran DDS at Clinica Dental Privada in Villa Real to be our preferred dentist. She is gentle but strong and has caught issues before they caused major problems and cost a lot of money.

Pharmacy

Although the pharmacies are not as large as Walgreens or Rite Aid, they stock the most common products needed. Many, but not all, prescription medications are available.

Narcotics is one area where you may experience issues when trying to obtain. Costa Rica has strict policies regarding narcotics, and many are not legal in the country. Some specialty medications may not have been approved in the country either.

All medication can be purchased on a per pill basis which can make the cost much more expensive. Medications such as Tylenol, Benadryl, Aspirin, etc., cost more than you would pay in the States. Some medications that require prescriptions in the States are available without a prescription and are cheaper. An example would be Oxa Forte 50/50mg (codeine + diclofenac), which is available without a prescription for around $1.50 per pill.

Tip → *If you are curious what medication will cost you and what is available, you can check the Fischel pharmacy website (http:// www.fischelenlinea.com) for availability and cost. Fischel is a pharmacy chain with locations throughout Costa Rica. If you have regular medications, be sure to speak to the pharmacist about your needs. Some pharmacists make limited trips to San José to pick up their stock. Even though they may have some of your prescriptions, pills are sold individually so they may not have a full month's supply if they don't anticipate a need.*

RECOMMENDATION

We have come to appreciate the service we have received from Pharmacist Dr. Ricardo Córdoba at Farmacia Tamarindo. They have ordered specialty medication for us as well as ensured they stock what we need on a regular basis. After our second or third visit, we were greeted by name whenever we entered the pharmacy. The personal touch and professional service make this our favorite pharmacy in town.

SCHOOLS

If you have children, one of your primary concerns about moving is probably schooling. We found the school options a bit difficult to research from afar. Many factors, such as the cost, the importance of English being offered, and how well your child fits in socially, need to be considered when it comes to schooling for your children. Now that we have been here for a while, we have a good understanding of what options are out there.

There are some common aspects of schooling in Costa Rica no matter what educational choice you make. For instance, all Costa Rican schools require school uniforms. Boys wear solid color pants with a collared shirt (either polo style or button down) in the school's color. Girls wear matching colors for top and bottom. The girls' tops are collared shirts, and the bottoms are skirts although some schools do allow the girls to wear pants instead of skirts.

Transportation to school is generally by chartered bus or van. Children who live close enough to school are allowed to walk or ride a bike. Other children are transported to school by their parents. Older students and especially college students may take the public buses primarily due to the longer distance to school. Cost for riding the bus varies by location.

Regardless of whether your children attend public, private, homeschool, etc., learning should not be limited to the classroom. We discovered that our children learned more from taking tours and experiencing the contrast of Costa Rica than they have from their standard curriculum. Getting out and hiking through the rainforest, wading in tide pools, and ziplining through the canopy have brought learning to life. These experiences have peaked the interest of our children and created a desire to research more about the sights, sounds, and smells of the environment.

School Records & Vaccinations

Prior to leaving the States, we made sure we had a CD copy of each of our children's entire school record. We also had their transcripts downloaded. (Complete school records and transcripts are two different things. A transcript is a report of performance including grade point average, courses, and credits. The complete record includes the transcript, attendance record, disciplinary actions, vaccines, and extracurricular activities for the student.)

Our daughter also needed to have all of her vaccines up to date. Remember you are not in the U.S. anymore. Costa Rica does not allow a choice about vaccines. They are mandatory through the government no matter your religion or personal views/beliefs, etc. The government is very strict about vaccines. If your child cannot have a vaccine due to a medical condition, you need to bring more information from the States. (Check with the Center for Disease Control (CDC) and The World Health Organization about what documentation you will need.)

Some schools even have vaccine days. In the States, the dentist would come into our child's preschool class and do small checkups and cleanings for the kids. We always had paperwork to fill out and an option to not have our child partake in the activities. This is not the case when it comes to vaccines in Costa Rica. It's not uncommon to have a doctor come into the school during the day, give the kids vaccines during school hours, and the parents not know anything about it until they pick their children up.

Public Schools

The public schools are taught completely in Spanish. If your children are able to handle this challenge, the local school system may be an option.

The schools are concrete buildings that have open windows in most classrooms. A very small amount of these schools have air-conditioning. Since it's hot and most schools don't have air-conditioning, school often starts early in the morning and is out by ten or eleven o'clock. As kids get older, classes run longer.

Most kids in Costa Rica graduate at the age of seventeen, much like graduating high school in the States. They then have an option to go on to what they call a university, where the student is able to pick what they want to study with more specialized instructions. You will see many young adults heading to school after dark since night school is very popular for young adults in Costa Rica.

Another consideration with public schooling is your children's plans for future education. If you believe they will want to attend college in the United States, Canada, or Europe, you may need to develop a high school plan to ensure they have all the credits necessary for admittance to their college of choice.

Keep in mind that Costa Rican schools have different calendar years than United States schools. If you are planning to return home for visits, this might impact your travels and availability of friends and family. Check with the school near your Costa Rican home for their calendar and start dates.

Our Story — School Research

Because schooling has always been a main concern for us, we read everything on the internet that we could find about schooling. We also read blogs that talked about kids and international moves and how the move will affect the child. This still left us with many questions about the Costa Rican public school systems, but from what we were reading, it looked like the schools were good.

Since all of our research showed that the public school system was decent, we planned to enroll our thirteen-year-old daughter in the system. Even though she could speak very little Spanish, we thought this would allow her to make friends and learn the language and cultures more quickly, and she seemed up to the challenge. (This is called full immersion.) However, our plan changed when we arrived in Costa Rica and started talking to the local expats and ticos.

We met many doctors, lawyers, dentists, and other successful people on the beach and struck up conversations with them about the school system. They told us not to put our children in the public school system, and the information they gave us raised a big red flag. We were not receiving confirmation that the system was as good as our internet research had led us to believe. Their responses put me on a mission to find out how the successful locals approached school.

We discovered that all of these people either had attended the private North-American-type schools (similar to those in the States) or had their kids in private school. Most of the families afforded private school through scholarship programs. (We are sure there are professionals out there that have attended Costa Rican public schools; however, we were not able to find any of these people to talk to.)

Since we wanted to make sure that we gave our children the best education possible, we took the public school system off the table.

Private School

A handful of private schools are here in the Tamarindo area and throughout most expat communities in Costa Rica. Some commonly known school programs can be found, such as International Baccalaureate (IB) and Waldorf. The cost can range from $2,500 to over $10,000 per student per year. Most private schools offer multiple student discounts and reduced tuition for cash payment up front. The majority of colleges in the United States accept the diplomas from most of these private schools; however, we recommend you check with the specific college to ensure acceptability.

Homeschool

One of the most popular options in Costa Rica is homeschooling. Several homeschool groups get together for study and/ or social interaction in the Tamarindo area plus Facebook groups, such as Guanacaste Homeschoolers Costa Rica, exist where you can connect with other parents to coordinate your efforts. Aside from the standard benefits of the homeschool option, such as curriculum choice and time management, a child's education is easily augmented with cultural experience by spending time out of the house and in the local community.

Online School

A similar but slightly different option from homeschooling is online school. Both public and private schools offer online programs. Just like the brick and mortar schools, each school has different benefits and drawbacks.

If you are planning on taking advantage of the online school option, there are some things to consider. One of the considerations is school supplies. (See the chapter on Shopping regarding what to purchase here.) Whether the school is public or private, the students will spend almost their entire school day on computers. That means the most important school supply they need is a computer. If the current computer is old or obsolete, it is a must to provide one that exceeds the bare minimum. Personally, we purchase new MacBook's for our children as part of their back-to-school shopping. We cannot stress enough that computers need to be purchased before leaving the States.

Another consideration is that regular school supplies are limited and pricey in Costa Rica. You may also experience difficulty in finding specific items needed for projects, such as science kits or bulky items for presentations. To address these issues, you may need to communicate with the teachers and get creative with developing alternatives. Request your school supply list as early as possible to reserve enough space and weight in your luggage to purchase supplies in the States and bring them back with you. (Get more information in the Shipping section of the Miscellaneous chapter.)

Our Story – School

We homeschooled one of our children the first year we arrived. As you know, we were planning on enrolling our daughter in a local public school as soon as we arrived here but quickly discovered it was not an option for our situation. One of our concerns was ensuring we met all the requirements for her to rejoin the United States school system should we ever need to move back. Another concern was her ability to get into college.

Our school system in Colorado required us to register as homeschooling our daughter, and she was required to take standardized testing since she was in the 7th grade. We discovered that the test did not need to be our specific state assessment but could be one from a different part of the United States. They also allowed us to designate a proctor to administer the test if we chose. The Costa Rican private school had teachers and individuals who would facilitate the test as the proctor and submit the results to the school district. To make things easy, we simply scheduled the testing for our summer visit immediately following the school year.

The school district also required that we track the number of hours our student spent on schoolwork. The total at the end of the year needed to be 280 hours. Although it may be possible to take advantage of this by saying her entire life is experiential learning, we wanted to make sure nothing would come back to bite us later. We kept a very detailed calendar and a log of the time our daughter actually spent in a book or on her computer doing schoolwork. We used an app and website called Duolingo for her Spanish studies, and a website called CK-12 provided her science instruction as well as other science experiments including growing local plants from seeds. (Thanks to this class we now have a mango tree!) Steve's mother is a math tutor who was familiar with grade level math curriculum and became our daughter's math teacher through Skype. In English class, she was required to read books and do book reports which we reviewed and went over for corrections. Physical Education was accomplished through snorkeling in the ocean and swimming in the pool. All time was accounted for.

To further protect ourselves from wasting our time on a year of education that would not be recognized, we joined the Home School Legal Defense Association. This group advocates for homeschoolers and their parents. Their website explains:

> "Seeing a need for affordable legal advocacy, the two Mikes (founders and lawyers) joined forces to establish a nonprofit ministry to defend and advance the constitutional right of parents to direct the education of their children and to protect family freedoms."

There is a fee for membership that we felt was reasonable to ensure her education was valid by anyone of importance.

Since our son was in high school when we moved, we did not feel we possessed the skills to complete his high school education in the homeschool setting and were concerned about how it would affect his future plans. After much research, we enrolled our son in a private online school called K-12 International Academy. This is a private international school with students around the globe. The cost is about $7,000 per year depending on the number of credits taken and payment arrangement.

Initially, our son struggled to succeed in this new learning environment. Coming from a high C average in his traditional public school, his grades dipped as he tried to find his feet. Once he gained some organizational skills and began to understand how the school worked, he exceeded his past performance. He was able to finish his senior year *four* months early with all A's and B's. We have a couple of proud parents right here!

Even though the online school provided the credits and accreditation needed for graduation and future educational opportunities, much of our son's learning took place outside this environment. From snorkeling, kayaking, hiking, socializing with locals and visitors from around the world, doing service projects like building homes, and experiencing the biodiversity that Costa Rica offers, he was able to augment his classroom learning with some invaluable life experience. We cannot stress enough the educational benefits of our move on our entire family.

Before starting our second year here we realized that it would be best for our family to look at other options rather than homeschool our daughter. Our home state offers a free online option through their school of choice. Since we maintain our residency in the States, we are able to access this free school option.

We are confident that because the online program is offered through the school system our daughter would not have any issues with returning to the States for further education now or after graduating from high school. The curriculum covers the same topics as the brick and mortar options, so if we moved back to the States, she should have no trouble joining her classmates in stride. Should she complete the program, the diploma is acceptable for college application as well.

Similar to the experience our son had, our daughter struggled to find her footing in the new online school environment. Initially, she was having trouble staying on top of what was due when. She would get confused and miss assignments at times. We now print out her schedule for each class and post it on her wall to check off and monitor her progress in each class. The parent portal allows us to track her grades and see how much time she spends in each class (assuming she is logged in when working on/studying).

We learned that we must not only help our children but also step back to let them learn time management and other skills. It took us retraining our thinking to realize and remind ourselves that their education will not resemble our own. Just as the workplace has changed since we were young, so have the skills needed in order to be successful. The online school environment seems to more directly resemble projects and tasks in today's workplace. By learning how to communicate and manage assignments online, our kids are gaining experience that will allow them to pursue jobs where they can work remotely at anytime anywhere.

INCOME

For many, the move to this new paradise can only be sustained by finding income to support the new life. Although you may show up with a nice nest egg from liquidating your life in the States, there is a good chance that life will happen and sooner or later the savings is not enough. At this point, it is time to find a job to restock the coffers.

Until you become a resident, you are not legally allowed to work in Costa Rica without a work visa. As a tourist, your options for income are extremely limited. It basically boils down to three options:

1. obtain employment using a work visa;
2. find a job that is willing to pay you through another country;
3. operate a business.

Two of your three options for employment in Costa Rica involve working for others. These two options are very different. The first involves receiving income in country through the use of a work visa. The second option is to obtain a position that is paid through a country outside of Costa Rica. This second approach has become, and continues to develop, as the primary way expats receive income.

Tip → *Contact an accountant in your home country along with any country that you receive income from to identify your tax liabilities and legal requirements.*

RECOMMENDATION

If you need assistance in moving your job online or establishing an e-commerce business, we recommend you contact Viva Purpose, an education and coaching firm designed to help you achieve your goals. In addition to establishing personalized action plans, they offer specialized training in e-commerce.

Work Visas

To legally receive income from a job in Costa Rica, you must be a resident or have a work visa. For many years this was not enforced and you would find people from all over the world working in virtually all varieties of businesses. It was not uncommon to walk into a restaurant owned by a German couple with an Argentinian waiter and a Canadian busboy, all on tourist visas. In recent years, immigration officers have begun to crack down on illegal workers. Random checks for employment regulation compliance are becoming much more common with fewer businesses taking the risk on undocumented workers.

To obtain a work visa, the business that wishes to employ an individual must file the request with the General Directorate of Immigration and Aliens. At times, a high level of expertise is required to justify the need for employing a foreigner. Most times it is the larger corporations that apply for work visas to staff their workforce. Just like any other country, Costa Rica is more concerned with employing its own citizens than providing opportunities for aliens. Work visas may be an option, but for most, you will need to find other sources of income.

Foreign Employer

Today, the most common method for expats to receive income prior to obtaining their residency is through foreign employment. Thanks to the internet and various telecommunications platforms, the virtual office has changed the way many support themselves. There are several online jobs in almost every field imaginable. High overhead costs of maintaining office space and increased telecommunications abilities, along with the transition to online shopping for products and services, have many companies turning to the virtual office for their employees.

To maximize your online opportunities, you will need to

be creative and disciplined. Consider your current position. Unless your position requires you to be physically face-to-face with your customer, you may be able to telecommute and be just as effective. It may require you doing the research and working to sell the idea to your employer. Should you try this method, remember to approach it from the side of benefits for the company. How will your telecommuting save or make them money, increase production, or increase efficiency? If you present a situation that is beneficial to all involved, the response could be life changing.

An alternate approach is to search for online positions currently available. Nearly all job boards or job search sites offer work-from-home or online opportunities. Use your skills and interests to choose the type of work you are interested in and apply, apply, apply. This may be a time for a transition into a new industry or simply modifying the way you perform the same type of work you have been doing for several years. There are certification programs and training offerings for multiple online opportunities. It may require an investment for credentials, but the freedom of working wherever you desire is priceless.

We have met many people who have found their niche in the e-commerce environment. As we mentioned, this is a huge market and appears to be the wave of the future for shopping. If you have the skills or the desire to learn them, e-commerce businesses can be major revenue producers. Just look at companies like Amazon, Uber, and Airbnb. Compare the net worth and growth of these companies with what you see from brick and mortar companies like Sears, Best Buy, and Kohl's. It is easy to see the trend moving to the online platform. There are several small stores that are capitalizing on this trend, and you could too.

Buying a Business

If you do not have an online job, a trust fund, or guaranteed income, you may consider purchasing a business. We must caution you that without providing tico jobs you may have issues. If you plan to operate a restaurant, don't expect to be able to run it yourself.

Although, as a tourist, you are able to receive earnings from the business, it is a bit of a gray area as to whether or not a tourist owner can do the physical work to produce the earnings. It seems the businesses that employ locals are appreciated and experience fewer issues with permits, etc., than those who try to support only expat homes. Remember, as tourists, we are guests in the country, so it would not be polite to put your host out of work.

Buying a business has many aspects, and we have provided some information and tips in the following sections to help you avoid some of the pitfalls of operating a business in Costa Rica. The use of an attorney, opening your own corporation, and verifying the books are a few of the major factors that can directly affect your business success.

Using an Attorney

Aside from the obvious need for an attorney to file the

papers transferring the business into your name, it is extremely beneficial to have an attorney review the business documents to ensure everything has been filed correctly and that there are no legal issues, current, past or future, which could jeopardize the business. Usually, the attorney has lived in the area and is knowledgeable about the history of the business. (Some businesses change ownership very frequently as people try to relocate only to find that this is not the place for them. The attorney may be able to use this history to assist you in avoiding the same pitfalls previous owners encountered.) If you are considering establishing a new business, an attorney is often able to inform you of risks you have not considered due to their understanding of not only the laws but also the culture.

Establishing and Using Your Own Corporation

The Guanacaste region has several businesses for sale. It is very easy to simply assume ownership of an existing corporation. Unless the current owners have other belongings, like their home, held in the corporation, they are usually willing to sell the corporation as is. They may even try to sell the idea to you as an "already established business with a good history." That sounds very attractive. Why try to start from scratch when you can just hit the ground running?

The primary reason that we would advise against assuming a corporation and to establish a new one is because of that very history. You have no way to protect yourself from someone placing a lien on the business for work completed on the business' behalf that occurred prior to your ownership. If there is an unpaid invoice from before your ownership, you may become liable for that too. By assuming the corporation, you are assuming all of its history, even the undisclosed issues. If you start with a fresh corporation, you limit your exposure to these risks as it is seen as a new business. There is rarely an issue with the trade name, and you should always negotiate copyright items. Once again, an attorney should be able to assist with this process.

Verifying Books

If you are attempting to gain ownership of an established business, it is important to know what you are buying. This concept is true no matter what country the business is located in. It is Business 101. Verifying the books sounds easy, right? It may not be so simple.

We have a background in finance and mortgages, and at times we have used unusual sources to verify income, etc. We have used bank statements, canceled checks, pay stubs, and bills showing payment received to ensure the accuracy of information given. We have a fairly open mind when it comes to verifying evidence, but some of the records provided have left us with insurmountable doubt and disappointment that the transaction could not continue.

Most small businesses in Costa Rica file taxes using Régimen De Tributación Simplificada (Rts). This form of taxation requires paying income tax based on the amount paid for purchased goods used to generate the product, not actual product sales amounts. Due to this type of tax reporting, copies of filed taxes are not a good estimation of business income. The filed taxes would only report how much was spent to generate the sales not the income from the sales themselves.

Another way to verify what you are buying is through the business' books. This is where we have had the most difficulty in confirming a business' value. Our experience has shown that many businesses do not keep good records. We have been provided Microsoft Excel spreadsheets for profit and losses with no evidence to support the numbers provided. Other times we have been given handwritten log books of sales where the daily log did not match up with reported sales and earnings. An increasing numbers of businesses have caught up to technology and are using computer programs to track inventory and sales, but many are still using old ledgers or spiral notebooks to keep their records.

Bank records can be an easy way to check that there is money coming into the business. Regular deposits should correlate to recent sales. By adding up these deposits, it is possible to assume that the income reported is actually being made by the business and deposited into the account. The issue we have seen regarding bank statements is a commingling of funds. As a tourist, it is more difficult to establish a personal checking account. (See the chapter about Money). Because of this, some business owners use their business accounts for personal use. When this happens, it is very difficult to separate what is personal from what is business. If there is no outside income, it may not be as much of an issue.

Whatever information is provided, be sure you are able to validate that information with another source. It may be handwritten log books with supporting bank statements. Or perhaps, Excel spreadsheets with purchase orders. You may need to be open-minded about the source of the information and the way it is presented, but in the end, it must convey a level of confidence that the risk is worth taking.

Opening a Corporation

You may be thinking to yourself "we have no need to open a corporation." Do you plan to own property? How are you planning on supporting yourself? Every long-term expat we've met that has successfully made the move and stayed for more than a couple years has established a corporation for one reason or another. Many are, in fact, business owners, but others simply needed an easy way to establish and/or transfer ownership of homes and even vehicles. (Although a corporation is not needed to own a vehicle, it is often an asset of a property or business).

We have opened a handful of small businesses in the United States, all of which we did on our own without the assistance of a lawyer. We have established sole-proprietor, partnership, and s-corp type businesses which all have similar processes with a few different forms. We can tell you that the process of establishing a corporation in Costa Rica is just as easy but will *always* require the assistance of an attorney. The forms submitted must be signed and stamped by an attorney to be accepted by the government.

Most towns and every city will have at least one, if not multiple, attorneys to choose from. If you cannot find one locally that you're happy with, perhaps try a nearby city for a larger pool of options. Our understanding is that all licensed attorneys can practice all types of law. That being said, we recommend you search for one that specializes in your need. If you are working on obtaining residency, you should find an attorney that specializes in residency. The same goes for criminal cases and real estate. All offices seem to be able to establish corporations and handle property transactions like real estate, vehicles, boats, etc.

Tip ➔ *All corporations must have at least one tico shareholder. The attorneys are able to take care of this requirement for you and explain the details.*

Corporation Cost

You may be thinking that opening a corporation is a pricey endeavor, but it can be relatively affordable. Depending on how much involvement you want from the attorney, your price will vary. We suggest interviewing a couple of attorneys to find one that is not only fairly priced but that you feel you can trust. Asking locals and expats for recommendations may save you some trouble and help you find the more reputable professionals.

Our Story — Corporation

We paid $1,000 USD to establish our corporation. The

entire startup process including establishing a bank account was completed in less than two weeks. The attorney's office we chose also takes care of the annual filing and maintains the books for about $300 per year. This is probably not the cheapest option, but we have come to trust our attorney and have experienced nothing but professional service. The forms the attorney prepares must be filed with the Costa Rican government in San Jose.

90-DAY BORDER RUNS

osta Rica offers different types of visas. Each type of visa has a different process for renewal. We will be discussing the *tourist visa* primarily since that is the one we have experience with at this point, and that is what all expats will start with until filing for residency. Costa Rican tourist visas are offered for a maximum of ninety days. At the end of the ninety days, you will be required to leave the country or risk being deported, jailed, fined, and possibly refused re-entry.

There are three common types of border controls: *immigration*, which checks people crossing the border; *customs*, which inspects goods crossing the border; and *security*, which verifies the safety of the vehicles crossing the border. The Immigration Office in many countries should more accurately be named the Migration office as it addresses both *immigration*, traveling or relocating *into/to* a new country, and *emigration* traveling or relocating *out of /from* one country to the next. Depending on which country you are visiting, current political conditions, and your mode of travel, you may experience any of these border controls.

Before getting into the details of border runs, we would first like to address a common misunderstanding. For Nicaraguan border crossings as a United States citizen, you don't have to stay out of Costa Rica for 72 hours. The 72-hour law applies to people who are transporting goods into the country and those holding passports from certain countries.

When entering Costa Rica from Nicaragua, the most common visa for holders of U.S. passports is a 90-day tourist stamp. When entering the country, you will need to have proof of onward travel within 90 days. This needs to be either a bus ticket or an airline ticket. The immigration officer is the one who has the discretion on how long your stamp will be good for. They can deny your entry for any reason, however, if you are following the rules, you should receive a 90-day stamp.

There are some differences in the process and regulations for crossing the border into Panama. If you are crossing at the Panama border, you will need onward travel back to the country that issued your passport. You will also need to provide proof of a bank account showing $500 in cash. When crossing into Panama, there is a three-hour wait until you can cross back over. We have not had an opportunity to cross the southern border but these details are what our research has provided.

Our Story — Onward Travel

One time, when we were returning from a mission trip to Nicaragua, the immigration officer would not accept our bus ticket, and he told us we needed to purchase bus tickets outside. We found one of our Spanish-speaking friends who asked to speak to his manager. We stood at the counter for over thirty minutes until he finally stamped our passport and away we went without ever speaking to the manager. When we got on the bus, we were informed that the people who had airline tickets but had not printed a hard copy were not allowed to enter either. They all went outside and bought $49 bus tickets. This was the only time we have ever had a problem with our proof of onward travel. Most times, we simply show them a ticket or itinerary on our phone, and they accept it.

At first, we bought bus tickets for our onward travel. Recently, we did a little more research with airline tickets. United Airlines will refund a ticket if it's canceled within twenty-four hours of purchase. We have used this method of onward travel on our last couple of crossings. This seems to be the easiest method of showing onward travel as long as you remember to take a printed copy of your itinerary in case an officer requests it and to cancel the ticket once you've crossed.

Border Crossing Cost

All payments must be in cash and in either the local currency or in dollars. If you are walking across the border, it is easiest to use U.S. dollars, but you may save a few cents if you pay with local currency.

Table 5 - Walking Border Crossing Fees

Walking Border Crossing Fees Nicaragua	
Costa Rica Exit Fee	$8.00
Costa Rica Border Zone Fee	$1.00
Nicaragua Entry Fee	$12.00
Nicaragua Exit Fee	$2.00
Nicaragua Border Zone Fee	$1.00
Total	$24.00

Table 6 - Airline Border Crossing Fees to U.S.

Airline Border Crossing Fees To U.S.	
Costa Rica Baggage Inspection Fee	$2.00
International Boarding Tax	$27.00
Costa Rica Transportation Tax	$12.10
Costa Rica Common Area User Charge	$3.58
Costa Rica Security Fee	$2.69
U.S. Transportation Tax	$18.00
U.S. APHIS User Fee	$3.96
U.S. Immigration User Fee	$7.00
U.S. Customs User Fee	$5.50

Tip → *Make sure you take cash in the form of U.S. dollars to complete the process. It is much easier than trying to provide the different forms of currency. Costa Ricans will not accept the Nicaraguan córdoba (valued around 3.3 U.S. cents requiring even more conversions on the fly) and the Nicaraguans will not accept Costa Rican colónes. United States dollars are the standard form of currency accepted at all stations of the border crossing.*

The other item we strongly suggest taking for border crossings is a pen. You will be required to complete immigration forms for both countries. You will have a better experience, and the people waiting in line will greatly appreciate you having the forms completed when you reach the counter.

The Process

We are visitors in Costa Rica and want to abide by its laws, so making sure we leave the country every ninety days is important. We make it a point to complete our crossings three to five days before our stamp expires to ensure that we don't overstay our visa due to unforeseen circumstances like road closures, weather, or personal issues. Most of these runs can be uneventful, and they only take half a day.

While the drive to Nicaragua is absolutely beautiful and we get to splurge on fast food as we pass through Liberia, it still causes great stress. We've spent many hours of research trying to prepare for our crossings. One of the things that have come up multiple times is that process time, length of time out of the country, and onward travel documentation required are at the discretion of the border officers.

The Parking Lot

As you approach the border, at about three miles out, you will encounter a line of trucks along the side of the road or blocking the lane of traffic. You need to pass all of these trucks and continue down the road to where the border parking lot is. You will pass by an inspection booth where the trucks are required to check in but you do not need to. You can continue on even if it means driving on the wrong side of the street. We know it sounds crazy, but that is the way it works. If you don't use the oncoming lane, being cautious to watch for oncoming vehicles, you will spend the majority of the day waiting for the trucks to move through the process.

From the moment you enter the parking lot, you will be approached by men offering to assist you in crossing the border. They will tell you that they can speed up the process and move you to the front of the line. Although they are being truthful and have probably worked out a bribe system with the official managing the flow at the office, it is not necessary to pay for their services. These men will be extremely assertive. They will try to hand you the forms to fill out for exiting Costa Rica. If you do not want to pay for their services, ***do not take the form.*** The men will charge you for providing the form, which is free at the border office. These same men will tell you they will watch your car. Once again, this is for a fee.

We make it clear up front that we do not require their assistance. We usually will offer one mil (1000 colónes) for watching our car. They always argue, and we always tell them that it is for less than one hour and that we don't need their service in the first place. Keep in mind that these men are not there in any official capacity. They are simply Costa Rican citizens trying to earn a living on the border. If you have trouble, insist that you are going to speak to a police officer, and they will usually back down.

Our Story — Border Parking

Several people are trying to make a buck at the border. This is something that makes our anxiety come back. From the minute you pull into the Border Zone, people will want to help you for a nice fee. The first time we pulled up, a guy pulled our passports out of our hands, and before we could say a word, he had filled out the paper for us to cross.

He then went on to inform us that it would be $60 a person so a total of $180 to cross. He continued to tell us this would include the "very high" border taxes that we needed to pay and the assistance of his friend who would help us get back across without waiting an extended time in Nicaragua. After a little exchange of some words, we made it very clear that we didn't need help in crossing.

We had no clue what we were doing, but we were not going to pay an extra $180 for someone to hold our hand. This was just another adventure that we were on. With what little Spanish we knew at the time, we were able to make it across and back into Costa Rica in less than 2 hours.

First Booth/Pay Station

After exiting your car, the first place you need to pay a fee is on the northwest corner of the parking lot. You walk down about ten steps to the booth where a cashier will collect the $8 Costa Rica Exit Tax. The cashier will give you a small piece of paper for a receipt. (We always hold onto everything given to us until we have completed the process just to be sure.) From there, you will walk back up the stairs and head north up the road to the Emigration Office.

Emigration Office: Costa Rica

This office is where you may have the longest wait both on your way out of Costa Rica and on the way back in. We try to make sure we arrive early to beat the buses full of passengers. Several people will ask you to exchange money and/or purchase telephone SIM cards. More men offering to assist you with crossing and front-of-the-line privileges will likely approach you as well. They are not lying; we have seen several people taken to the front of the line where the Emigration Officer guarding the door lets them pass the crowd. If the line is long and you have more money than time, this may be an option.

You will need to get a copy of the Emigration Form to complete in order to get your exit stamp. There is no fee paid at this office. Once you reach the counter, the Emigration Officer will take the form, inspect your passport, and scan it into the system. Assuming everything checks out and you have no outstanding warrants, etc., they will place the exit stamp in your passport.

Our Story — Border Restrooms

Often we drive straight to the border and don't stop for gas or coffee. At this step of the process, we recommend if anyone in your group needs to use a bathroom to do so now. The facilities at the Costa Rica Emigration Office are clean and have running water for both the sinks and the toilets. These facilities are also free. When you enter the restroom, there is a utility closet where someone is usually handing out little amounts of toilet paper. If no one is there, they will leave a box next to the door. Carrying hand sanitizer is a good idea because they have always been out of soap.

The next opportunity for restroom services is in Nicaragua. These restrooms are located to the left of the doors at the entrance of the Nicaraguan Immigration Office. When Nikki and our daughter used the ladies facilities on the Nicaragua side, they had to pay to use the restroom. It only cost a couple of cents; however, this could be a problem if you don't have the correct currency.

The facilities were also very dirty. During Nikki's visit, the sinks and toilets were in place but without running water. A lady at the door collected the money and handed out a small amount of toilet paper. From what Nikki understood with the little Spanish she knew, the lady said that if they needed more toilet paper they could get some, but it was going to cost.

Once they finished, the woman was there ready to clean up. She dipped a modified three-liter plastic bottle into a trashcan full of water and stepped into the stall. She threw the water toward the back of the toilet in order to flush it. You can imagine the water going everywhere! The water cascaded down the wall where the toilet collected enough for flushing. As Nikki stepped out of the stall, the woman turned around and offered to wash her hands with the little bit of water that was left. The water that made it past the toilet finished its path down the wall to the floor. The woman then swept the water that dripped off the walls out of the stall, through the restroom, and out onto the street. If you want a memorable experience, the Nicaraguan border restroom is a very affordable option, but we will choose to stop in Costa Rica first!

Exit Count Station

From the Emigration Office, you will walk down the right side of the road to a passport inspection checkpoint where a Costa Rican police officer will inspect your passport and check for the exit stamp from the Emigration Office. This checkpoint is immediately prior to the border. You will continue on from there to the first Nicaraguan checkpoint where they will give you a piece of paper with the number of people from each passport country in your party. Once you leave this checkpoint, you can cross the road where there is a wider walkway away from traffic and continue on to the Border Zone and Immigration Office of Nicaragua.

Border Zone Booth: Costa Rica

You will approach a marketplace where several Nicaraguans sell various goods and food. This is a decent place to pick up some souvenirs if you would like something from Nicaragua. We have sampled some of the foods and snacks, and most are pretty good at a fairly reasonable price. At the north end of the market area, you will see a building, which is the Immigration Office. You will need to enter that building for your next checkpoint. Immediately inside the glass doors, there is a booth where a cashier will collect your Border Zone Fee of $1. You will receive another small paper receipt along with the immigration form for Nicaragua. From here, you will simply get in line for immigration into Nicaragua.

Immigration Office: Nicaragua

The immigration officer will take the completed immigration form, inspect your passport, and scan everything into the system. The officer will collect the $12 entry fee and ask you questions about your reasons for entering Nicaragua. They will want to know how long you are planning on staying and if it is for tourism or business.

As a result of having multiple occupations and reasons for travel, we have provided various answers to these questions. Most times we have responded that we are simply vacationing and are not sure how long we will be staying but possibly a couple days. On some occasions, we have told them we are crossing the border to renew our tourist visa in Costa Rica. Depending on the agent, they may try to tell you that you must stay a certain amount of time ranging from hours to a couple days in Nicaragua. Others scan, collect, stamp, and pass you through. To us, it is clear that there is not sufficient training for these workers on the laws of entering and leaving. Or it may just be part of the corruption where they are trying to help their buddies collect extra fees for "expediting" your crossing without the wait.

Remember, unless you have an outstanding warrant, you are not breaking any laws leaving or entering a country. These officers are trying to protect the citizens of their prospective countries from foreigners who may wish to do them harm. The way you respond tells them how to ascertain your intentions and whether or not to give you a visa, what type of visa, and for how long.

Once you have completed the requirements of this station, you will continue on to the Nicaragua side through another set of glass doors. If you are bringing any baggage with you, there is a conveyor belt you will need to load them onto which feeds them into the scan machine. If the officers feel a duty is owed for goods in your luggage, this is where you will be asked to pay it. Once you collect your bags, or if you didn't have any, you will exit the building to the right.

Border Zone Booth: Nicaragua

As you exit the glass doors, you will be greeted by another crowd of people, this time Nicaraguans, trying to sell you stuff and get you to pay for assistance. Every time we walk out those doors, we have had people tell us that we have to stay in Nicaragua or we won't be allowed back into Costa Rica. Every time, except for one, we walked right back into the Emigration Office of Nicaragua and continued through the process back into Costa Rica without issue. (We will discuss that encounter in the section titled Held Hostage in Nicaragua.)

From the exit of the Immigration Office to the entrance of the Emigration Office is a distance of about ten yards. You will enter the door to the right and immediately inside the doors is another Border Zone Booth. You will pay the Border Zone Fee of $1 to continue through the Border Zone back to Costa Rica.

Emigration Office: Nicaragua

Once you've received yet another paper receipt, you will go through the line to the Emigration Officer of Nicaragua. The officer will ask for your passport, and you will be required to pay the $2 Nicaragua Exit fee. On most occasions this is a quick inspect, pay, stamp process with little to no conversation. We have only had issues at this station one time when we were "held hostage in Nicaragua."

Immigration Office: Costa Rica

The Immigration Office is the last checkpoint of the border crossing. There are no fees at this office. The most important thing about this station is that you will need your proof of onward travel. Although we are usually able to pass through with a digital receipt or picture of the itinerary, there has been an occasion where they required a printed copy.

Most times we have been asked how long we plan on staying in Costa Rica. Your answer and the date of your onward travel will determine the number of days the agent authorizes in your passport. They are not required to give you ninety days. If your onward travel says you're leaving in ten days, that may be how many days they authorize. We always double-check that they give us the full ninety days.

If you have luggage, you will pass through customs on your way out of the building. Once you have cleared customs, the only things left are settling with the parking attendants where you will need to be firm, and the ride home. There is one road checkpoint around a half mile from the border where you may be stopped. They are only interested in whether you took the vehicle out of the country. If not, they will wave you past.

Our Story — Held Hostage in Nicaragua

So far, we have experienced the corruption we were warned about only one time while crossing. It happened on the Nicaraguan side. As we mentioned earlier, the trouble began just outside the Immigration Office of Nicaragua checkpoint. We stepped out the glass doors where we were amazed that for the first time we were not overrun with people trying to hand us the immigration form for Costa Rica, for a fee, of course.

As we approached the door to enter the Border Zone, we were told by a random Nicaraguan man that we had to wait in Nicaragua for five hours. We argued for a few minutes since he was blocking our entrance into the office. He told us we could skip the time if we paid $20 per person. From our research and past crossings, we knew this was not true. We insisted he tell us when the rules changed, but he just kept asserting that we pay or wait. Finally, a Nicaraguan border patrol agent opened the door, said something to the man to get him to leave us alone, and ushered us to the Border Zone Booth.

The agent gestured to come to his line when we were finished paying the Border Zone Fee. We thought we were saved. We incorrectly assumed that the agent was correcting the man outside and not simply telling him "I've got it." When we approached the booth, he took our passports, completed the paperwork, and then asked for $60 for the three of us. In shock, it took us a second to process what had happened. We tried to explain that we had never paid that much before and that it was always $2 each. He said it was because we didn't wait five hours in Nicaragua. We asked him to show us where the law had changed. The agent showed no indication he was going to budge on the bribe or justify the fee.

Using our past experience, we knew how much the fees should total and only had a small amount of cash in case we wanted to grab a cold drink at the border market. Steve had left our debit card at home, and our credit card does not allow cash advances. We did not have the $60 the agent was asking for. Steve showed him that we did not have enough. He gestured toward the ATM, and Steve told him he didn't have his bank card. After maintaining the standstill a few more minutes, he decided he would settle for all the cash we had on hand, so he dropped the price to $10 each. After a short discussion, we decided that we did not want to stay in Nicaragua any longer that day, so we coughed up the $30.

Since we had not actually crossed into the Border Zone, we were still in Nicaragua. It was not a Costa Rican border agent telling us we were not allowed to come into their country. After calming down, we also realized that it was not Costa Rica keeping us out for five hours or whatever amount of time. It was Nicaragua keeping us in. They were the ones asking us to buy our way out. That is why we have come to the realization that for a brief twenty minutes we were hostages of Nicaragua whose agents were demanding a ransom of $60.

As we left the building, the same random Nicaraguan gentleman greeted us, demanding we owed him money. We made it clear that we had paid the agent at the Emigration Office the bribe they were demanding. He followed us and raised his voice along the way, so we began to yell back and make it clear in no uncertain terms that he was not going to receive anything. He did not stop until we started asking for a police officer. At this point, he backed off, and we walked away and stewed about our experience the whole way back across the border.

Mail and Shipping

When we decided to come to Costa Rica, we had to decide what to do with our United States mail. Although over time much of the mail, especially junk mail, diminishes, there is still a need to maintain a way to receive mail correspondence. This is especially true if someone is receiving benefits, banking services, financial reports, etc. People handle this in many ways with the most common ways being using family members or virtual mailboxes.

Many people use a friend's or family member's address or possibly a post office box. They have someone screen their mail and scan in important correspondence that needs an immediate response. Our family established a system of what gets opened, what gets forwarded, and what gets shredded. From time to time, we call home and discuss what mail has arrived for us and how it should be addressed.

Others use a virtual mailbox service. Some of these services allow you to maintain a unique physical address in the States that is helpful for maintaining your residency, driver's license, etc.

Your mail is then sent and sorted according to your preferences. A few examples of these services would be Mailbox Etc., Jetbox, Aerocasilla, Traveling Mailbox, and Box Correos. This option may be preferred if you have snoopy relatives.

That covers your mail back in the U.S., but what about mail in Costa Rica? While it is possible to receive letters, packages, etc., in Costa Rica, it is very expensive and can be challenging logistically as well.

To give you an idea of shipping costs, we have provided six examples of shipping costs for online orders to Costa Rica.

Table 7 - Amazon Shipment Fees

Purchase	1	2	3
Item Cost	$29	$163.43	$197.03
Shipping and Handling	$21.99	$162.82	$64.68
Import Fee Deposit*			$70.23
Total	$50.99	$326.25	$331.94

Purchase	4	5	6
Item Cost	$197.70	$108.93	$1045.97
Shipping and Handling	$263.53	$281.55	$974.72
Import Fee Deposit*	$102.56	$82.67	
Total	$563.79	$473.15	$2020.69

*The Import Fee Deposit is collected by Amazon.
See Amazon's policy for details on this item.

Another interesting aspect of receiving mail and packages is the lack of addresses like in the States. Outside of San Jose, there are very few street names and addresses. The major roads connecting towns have names or numbers, but once you turn off the main road, the names disappear, and signs are unheard of. If there is a street name, very few people know it. Obviously, this makes for a challenge when addressing the mail, and depending on who is delivering it, when or if it will be received. A common address would be:

Figure 5 - Typical Costa Rican Address

Casa Roca
1 km al oeste y 500 norte de
Zona Industrial Zeta, complejo
de bodegas a mano derecha.
De la antigua pulpería

English translation:
Casa Roca
1 km to the west and 500 north
of Industrial Zone Zeta, complex
of wineries on the right-hand side.
From the old grocery store

Basically, you write the name of the house or business followed by directions using landmarks and other well know businesses or buildings. This style of addressing is challenging not only for mail but also when visiting friends for the first time.

Our Story — Shipping

During our first month in Costa Rica, family members wanted to send some things to the kids. We had informed everyone this was not an option. One of our family members was an Amazon Prime member. When she talked to customer service, Amazon assured her that she could ship things to Costa Rica with no additional fees because she was a Prime member. We expressed our doubt to her that we didn't believe this was the case, but Amazon told her differently.

Since she had been reassured multiple times that we wouldn't have to pay the extra fees, we decided on what we wanted to be shipped from the States. The Amazon representative worked with us for two days trying to get our order together. If we found an item that could not be shipped to Costa Rica, the representative would help find an equal item that could be shipped. This shipment had many things from pool stuff to a small hand mixer. After our order was placed and finalized, the representative quickly realized that she was wrong and there was going to be international shipping and taxes. This was a big disappointment to all of us, but we decided to continue with the order.

Not having an address didn't seem to be a problem. We used only the name of the house and landmarks around us. It took fourteen days for our stuff to arrive. A big truck with no markings pulled up outside our home and honked the horn. Two guys hopped out and opened up the back door of the truck revealing many boxes of all shapes and sizes. The loader handed a clipboard over to be signed and unloaded the boxes off the truck. If it was not for the fees, this would be a very easy way to have things shipped.

Social Media and News

The internet is everywhere! Although it is a blessing to be able to communicate with friends and loved ones back home or around the world, we would like to caution about the risks associated with sources of information.

The 2016 United States Presidential Election was quite the spectacle. As citizens, we felt it was important to do our civic duty and vote. In order to vote, we felt we needed to stay up to date on the candidates and issues. What we didn't expect was how much our view would be shaped by the social media posts of our friends and acquaintances (where the accuracy of information varied).

You often hear about news reports being biased or only telling part of the story. When it comes to the information from social media, this behavior is compounded to an infinite degree. It wasn't until we took a trip back to the U.S. for a visit that we were able to get some clarity on issues and candidates and see how much our views had been skewed by the posts of our social media contacts. We were still at the mercy of the media for accurate information, but it wasn't being filtered by the opinions and agenda of our friends.

Of course, one way to get quality accurate information is through online research. Every reputable news source has an online presence, and their information is accessible. The trouble is you have to be active in researching and discovering the information you want. When it comes to our news sources, we err on the side of being passive. This could be part of the stress-free lifestyle we are trying to pursue, but it becomes problematic when trying to take care of responsibilities, such as voting. We often only hear about news stories from the posts of our online contacts. We have limited U.S. television news reports based out of Florida and some national stations, such as CNN. For local news related to our home state, we simply know what our friends want to share. In order to establish proper viewpoints on issues and make responsible decisions, we must be proactive in gathering information of value.

Restaurants

Although Costa Rica is not known for its cuisine, there is a good chance you are going to eat out from time to time. In the following paragraphs, we decided to share some differences in the dining experience here versus dining in the States.

The first difference we noticed when we ate at a Costa Rican restaurant was that the food did not all come at the same time. We gave it little thought at the time but have come to find out that it is customary for the food to be delivered to the table as it is ready. Food is delivered while it's hot because the kitchens do not use heating lamps, and they are often small with little room to store plates that are ready.

We used to wait until the last person's food was on the table before we started eating. Sure, that's the polite thing to do in other places, but here, we just dig in. At first, it was uncomfortable eating while our friends or family members hadn't been served yet. We quickly moved past the uncomfortable feeling and have embraced the experience of enjoying our food at its finest.

The second thing that stood out at our first dinner was that it took us a long time to get the bill. We were enjoying the excitement of being fresh in the country, so we didn't notice right away. We kept talking and taking in the sights as we waited and waited for the check to be delivered to the table. Finally, we asked for the bill, and it was delivered.

What we have come to understand is that the servers do not bring the bill until you ask for it. In Costa Rica, meals are a special time to spend with your family and friends. Because the culture appreciates the value of mealtimes and the slower pace of life, they allow for it to continue as long as possible. For these reasons, they withhold the bill or "cuenta" in Spanish.

Unlike some of our dining experiences in the U.S., we have never felt rushed or as if the restaurant wanted the table for the next customer. Our meal always seems important here. We have sat for long stretches of time between ordering drinks or food without any pressure to wrap it up. On other occasions, we have sat at the table as all the others filled and there were none available for those waiting at the door. We still had to wait until we asked for the cuenta (bill) to be delivered.

The third difference is the "Service Charge" on the bill.

The 10% charge is intended to be split between the entire staff — server, bartender, cooks, etc. It is your discretion if you choose to tip above this amount. It is not necessarily expected but not uncommon either. There are no real guidelines here aside from showing gratitude as it is due.

RECOMMENDATIONS

We have a few must-try restaurant recommendations for those new to town or simply visiting.

Nogui's — We recommend making sunset reservations on the beach and enjoy a Piña Pie a la mode. This delicious delight features a sweet crunchy crust with the sweet fresh pineapple complemented by the vanilla ice cream. The pie takes the sunset to a whole new level.

Mandarina — While strolling main street shopping for that certain something, cool off with a Coco Milkshake from Mandarina. They have two locations in Tamarindo, and these milkshakes remind us that we live in paradise.

Surf Shack — Fresh out of the surf or missing home, sometimes you just need a burger and fries. The mouthwatering flavors of these big burgers hit the spot with crispy fries that complement it perfectly or are a great snack on their own.

Las Palmas (Villa Real) — For authentic Costa Rican cuisine, this is the place. The cafeteria style allows you to choose your salad, protein, and sides based on their appearance. It is a great way to try different types of Costa Rican dishes at an affordable price. We highly recommend the fried yuca.

Surf Club Sports Bar (Langosta) — This joint offers a super tranquillo (Spanish for tranquil or chill) family sports bar. You can throw some horseshoes, challenge someone at ping-pong, or enjoy several other games. While watching the best sports and games on the various televisions, you can throw back some drinks with the tastiest onion rings in Guanacaste.

Jalapeños (Playa Negra) — For the best burritos and nachos in Guanacaste, take a trip to Jalapeños restaurant in Playa Negra. For you surfers out there, this is a great way to refuel after an incredible session. These filling portions are packed with flavors and are complemented by some amazing smoothie options.

FINAL THOUGHTS

As we mentioned in the beginning, moving to Costa Rica was a drastic change for our family. Leaving our friends and family was difficult and especially hard for our children. Without speaking Spanish, meeting new people and making friends has taken longer and been more difficult. Some locals do not invest in friendships until the other person has lived here in Costa Rica for at least a couple years. The environment has ruined many more personal items than we were prepared for. In addition to the items, our bodies have taken a long time to adjust to the difference in temperature and humidity. As you can see, it is not always sunny here in paradise.

While certain parts of our move have been extremely challenging, we have enjoyed the metamorphosis that has taken place in our lives. We have developed deeper relationships and experienced many wonders. The struggles and challenges we have faced have brought us closer together as a family. We believe our choices have provided learning opportunities that will reap benefits throughout the lives of our children. If anyone were to ask, we would say that this move has been absolutely worth the cost and sacrifices necessary to accomplish it.

It is our hope that you were able to glean some information that will be useful in embarking on your journey. We wish to leave you with these blessings:

- *May your efforts be effective and produce amazing results.*
- *May you overcome the obstacles that block your path to true happiness.*
- *May your lives be ever enriched as you challenge your current boundaries.*
- *May you experience authentic "Pura Vida."*
  (Pura vida, literally translated "pure life" is a common greeting and farewell offered in Costa Rica.)

GLOSSARY OF TERMS

Caja
> 1. Register or checkout
> 2. Box
> 3. The national health care system administered by the Costarricense de Seguro   Social (CCSS)

Carnicería
> Butcher's shop; These meat shops offer fresh beef, poultry, and pork.

Cedula
> Costa Rican ID card issued to residents allowing them access to Caja and other government programs.

Certification De Flujo Proyectado
> Projected Flow Certification provided by an accountant to report estimated income and source of funds.

Colóne
> The currency of Costa Rica with a 2017 value of around ₡570 to $1.

Cuenta
> 1. Count

2. Account
3. Bill
4. Check
5. Total
6. Estimate

Emigration

Traveling or relocating *out of /from* one country to the next.

Expat

People living in one country with citizenship from another.

Feria

Fair, market. These markets are open-air areas that may have multiple vendors selling various goods. The term is also used in reference to the festivals that often include a rodeo and carnival.

Gringo / gringa

(male) (female)

A person, especially an American, who is not Hispanic or Latino

Immigration

Traveling or relocating *into/to* a different country

Llenar

Spanish word for "fill"

Mamon chino

A fruit also known as rambutan. The red part is a shell, similar in thickness to an orange peel but with hairy spikes. It splits in half when you press the center and reveals a white, jelly-like inside with a brown pit. It tastes similar to a pear.

Maracuyá

Green, reddish, golden tropical fruit in the passion fruit family. The pulp of maracuyá has a thin golden layer and another white one that protects the internal seeds. The black seeds are covered by an orange jelly, which is juicy and bittersweet and tastes like pineapple or guayaba.

Marchamo

Annual registration and taxes due in December for all street legal vehicles.

Mercado

A market. Could be any type of market but is generally used to indicate the larger stores.

Mil

1,000 in Spanish

Pilas

Large concrete or tile sinks used for washing clothing and dirty jobs.

Pura vida

Literally translated "pure life" and is a common greeting and farewell offered in Costa Rica

Régimen De Tributación Simplificada (Rts)

Form of taxation that requires paying income tax based on the amount paid for purchased goods used to generate the product, not actual product sales amounts

RETIVE (RTV)
Annual vehicle inspection required on all street-legal vehicles in Costa Rica

Tarjeta de circulación
Registration card

Titulo de propiedad
Property title

Transito
Traffic officer

WEBSITES

Amada Robles at Tamarindo Wellness Center
htt ps://www.facebook.com/tamarindowellnesscenter/

Amazon's policy
htt ps://www.amazon.com/gp/help/customer/display.html/?no-deId=201117970

Beachside Clinic
htt ps://www.facebook.com/beachsideclinic/

Beauty Clinic
htt ps://www.facebook.com/hbclinicscr/

Center for Disease Control (CDC)
htt ps://wwwnc.cdc.gov/travel/desti nati ons/traveler/none/cos-ta-rica

Centro De Carnes Villa Mar
htt ps://www.facebook.com/pages/Centro-De-Carnes-Villa-mar/227457084337229

CK-12
http://www.ck12.org/book/CK-12-Earth-Science-Concepts-For-Middle-School/

Claro
http://www.claro.cr/portal/cr/pc/personas/internet/

COSEVI (the Costa Rican equivalent of the DMV)
http://crtraveling.com/getting-costa-rican-drivers-license COSEVI

Costa Rican Embassy in Washington DC
http://www.costarica-embassy.org/index.php?q=node%2F111

Duolingo
https://www.duolingo.com/

Fischel pharmacy
http://www.fischelenlinea.com

General Directorate of Immigration and Aliens.
http://www.migracion.go.cr/extranjeros/visas.html

Home School Legal Defense Association
https://www.hslda.org/abou/index.html

Jalapeños (Playa Negra)
http://www.playanegrasurflodge.com/jalapeno

K-12 International Academy
http://www.icademy.com/

Las Palmas (Villa Real)
https://www.facebook.com/sodalaspalmas/

Mandarina
https://www.facebook.com/mandarinajuicebar/

Marchamo amount INS website Marchamo section
http://www.ins-cr.com/?iframe=true&width=85%&height=85%

Marchamo payment MOPT Ministry of Transit
http://www.mopt.go.cr/?iframe=true&width=85%&height=85%

Nogui's
http://noguistamarindo.com/

Pharmacist Dr. Ricardo Córdoba at **Farmacia Tamarindo**
https://www.facebook.com/farmaciatamarindo/

RPM Vacation Rentals
http://www.rpmvacationrentals.com/

RTV official website
http://www.rtv.co.cr/en/

Stacey Watson at **ReMax Ocean Surf & Sun**
http://www.remax-oceansurf-cr.com/our-agents

Surf Club Sports Bar (Langosta)
https://www.facebook.com/mkld/

Surf Shack
https://www.facebook.com/surfshacktamarindo/

Viva Purpose
http://vivapurpose.com/

World Health Organization
http://www.who.int/en/

More Resources
(for those who are serious)

Resource #1:

The instruction and information you NEED to make a successful international relocation.

Flight-plan Training covers the most pressing topics including preparing for the move, money, housing, transportation, healthcare,visas, and much more.

Discover the Flight-plan Training and develop the skills and dreams. Flight-plan Training is a 3-Month course with 8-weeks of online classes that are designed for you to work on your own time.

https://cutthecrapcostarica.com/product/flight-plan-training/

Resource #2:

Establish your finances with the Cut The Crap & Move To Costa Rica Budget.

This Xcel spreadsheet allows you to enter your informationinto a personalized budget for your move to Costa Rica. Included create are sample average monthly expenses for a couple living in Costa Rica. These expenses will fluctuate depending on the size, location, and amenities of your home. We have provided amounts that we feel most accurately report the average for expats living in conditions most similar to North America.

https://cutthecrapcostarica.com/product/cut-the-crap-move-to-costa-rica-budget/

Resource #3:

Not sure what to bring? This download-able Packing List to help you "Cut The Crap".

We provide the must-have items to make you feel at home in your new surroundings. We have tried and tested these products and use them ourselves. We provide links where you can easily locate and order the products for yourself. Make packing easier with our recommended Packing List.

https://cutthecrapcostarica.com/product/cut-the-crap-move-to-costa-rica-packing-list-2/

Resource #4:

Cut The Crap & Move To Costa Rica – Complete Download Tools & Resources

Downloadable content and tools to help you "Cut The Crap & Move To Costa Rica".

* Customizable budget to help you prepare to relocate to Costa Rica.
* Packing list to assist in preparations for moving to Costa Rica.

https://cutthecrapcostarica.com/product/cut-the-crap-move-to-costa-rica-complete-download-tools-resources/

Other Products

Premium Costa Rica Calendar

A beautiful 2019 Costa Rican calendar featuring gorgeous beaches, vibrant wildlife, and stunning landscapes.

A beautiful 2019 Costa Rican calendar featuring gorgeous beaches, vibrant wildlife, and stunning landscapes. With award-winning photos, this calendar is sure to be a great addition to any home or office!

https://cutthecrapcostarica.com/product/costa-rica-12-month-calendar/

eBook

Cut the Crap & Move to Costa Rica - eBook is perfect for on the go reading.

With active hyper-links! This allows you to click straight to any of the websites and references listed in the book. Download it to your phones e-reader and take this resource with you everywhere.

https://cutthecrapcostarica.com/product/cut-the-crap-move-to-costa-rica-ebook/

Hardcover

If your looking for a quality version of this great resource then look no further. The hardcover has a great feel. It makes a great gift idea too.

https://cutthecrapcostarica.com/product/cut-the-crap-move-to-costa-rica-paperback/

Made in United States
North Haven, CT
18 June 2022

20392644R00104